Stratford Ontario in Colour Photos, Saving Our History One Photo at a Time

Photography
by Barbara Raué
2013

Series Name:
Cruising Ontario

Book 56: Stratford

Cover photo: Stratford Civic Square

Series Name: Cruising Ontario
Saving Our History One Photo at a Time

Photos now in full colour
Check the Appendixes in the back of each book for
descriptions of architectural terms and building styles

Book 33: Southampton
Book 34: Jarvis
Book 35: Hagersville
Book 37: Simcoe
Book 38: Cambridge Part 1 – Galt Book 1
Book 39: Cambridge Part 1 – Galt Book 2
Book 40: Cambridge Part 2 – Preston
Book 41: Cambridge Part 3 – Hespeler
Book 42: Kitchener Book 1
Book 43: Kitchener Book 2
Book 46: Shelburne
Book 47: Alton, Mono and Caledon
Book 48: London in Colour
Book 50: Orangeville Beginnings in Colour
Book 51: Orangeville on Broadway in Colour
Book 52: Orangeville Book 3 in Colour
Book 53: Dundas in Colour Book 1
Book 54: Dundas in Colour Book 2
Book 55: Dundas in Colour Book 3
Book 56: Stratford
Book 57: Hanover

Other Books by Barbara Raue

Coins of Gold

Arrows, Indians and Love

The Life and Times of Barbara
Volume 1: Inventions That Have Enhanced My Life
Volume 2: Entertainment That I Have Enjoyed
Volume 3: East Coast Trips
Volume 4: Olympics Have Always Intrigued Me
Volume 5: Wonders of the World
Volume 6: Caribbean Cruises We Have Enjoyed
Volume 7: Animals
Volume 8: Storms and Other Major Disasters in My Lifetime
Volume 9: Wars, Terrorist Attacks and Major Disasters

The Cromwell Family Book

Visit Barbara's website to view all of her books
http://barbararaue.ericraue.com

Stratford

Stratford is a city on the Avon River in Perth County in southwestern Ontario located at the junction of Highways 7-8 and 19. When the area was first settled by Europeans in 1832, the town site and the river were named after Stratford-upon-Avon, England.

In 1832, the Canada Company, a large private land settlement agency, initiated the development of "Little Thames" as the market centre for the eastern Huron Tract. By 1834, a tavern, sawmill, and gristmill were built and a year later a post office called Stratford was opened. With the coming of the railroad in the 1850s and the designation of Stratford as county town, the village was transformed into a thriving administrative and commercial centre. Railway repair yards were opened here in 1871, and the town continued to expand. By 1885, Stratford had a population of 9,000 and it was incorporated as a city.

Furniture manufacturing became an important part of the local economy by the twentieth century.

The town is well known for being the home of the Stratford Shakespeare Festival which began in 1953. The annual festival brings hundreds of thousands of theatre goers and tourists to the area. The world-renowned festival takes place in four theatres throughout the city: the Festival Theatre, the Avon Theatre, Tom Patterson Theatre and the Studio Theatre.

The swan has become a symbol of the city. Each year twenty-four white swans and two black swans are released into the Avon River.

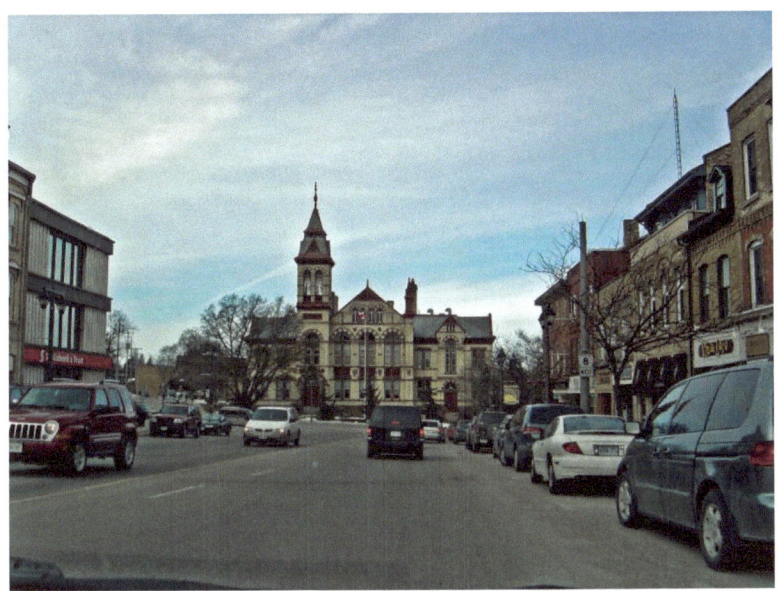

Stratford City Hall at the end of the street

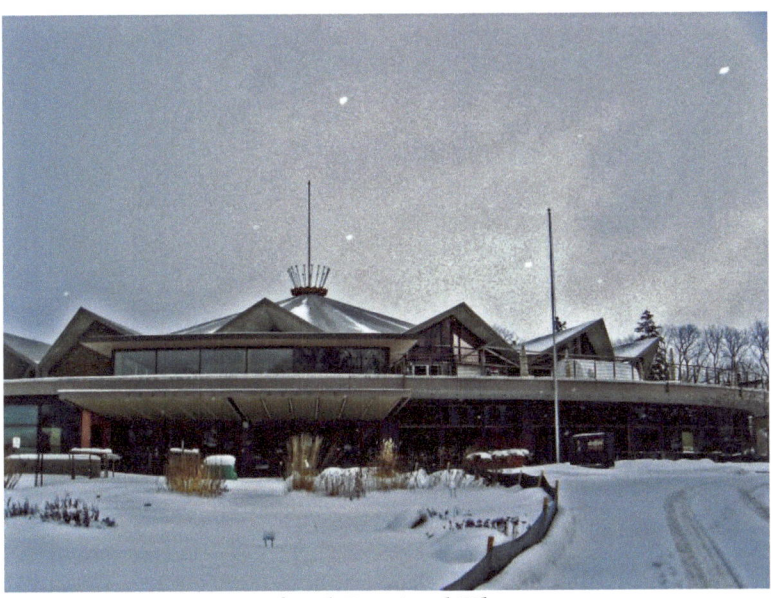

Stratford Festival Theatre

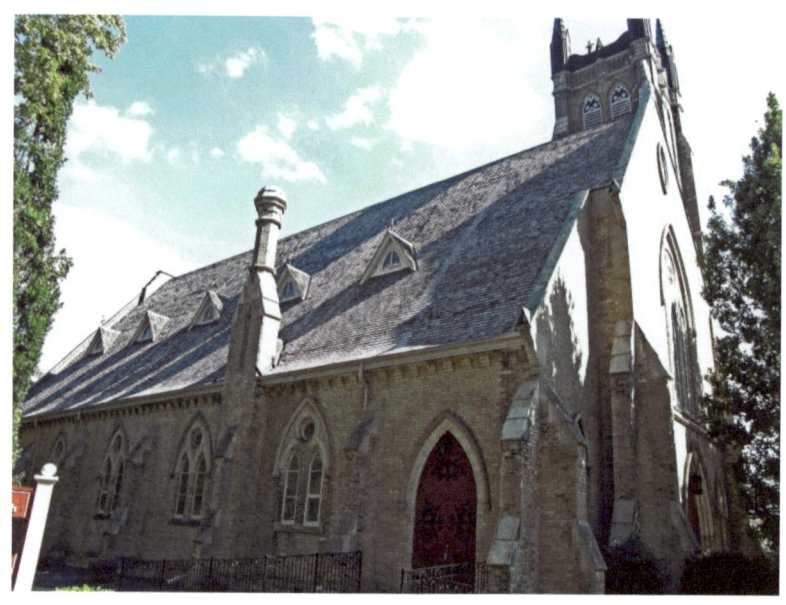

41 Mornington Street - St. James' Anglican Church – built in 1870, Gothic style, lancet windows, buttresses, bell tower

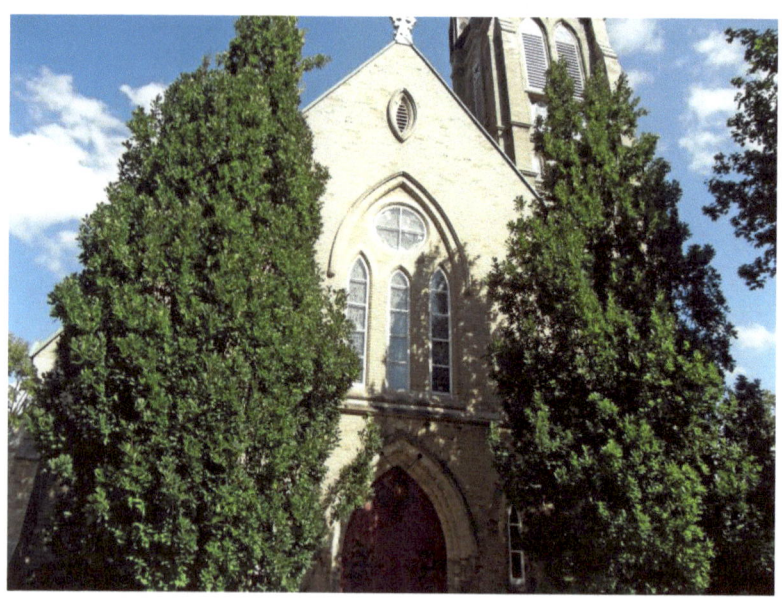

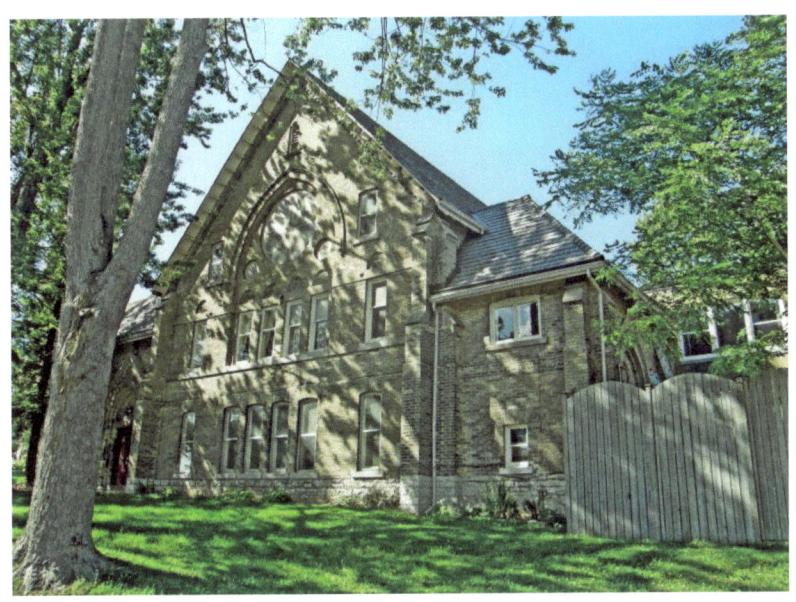

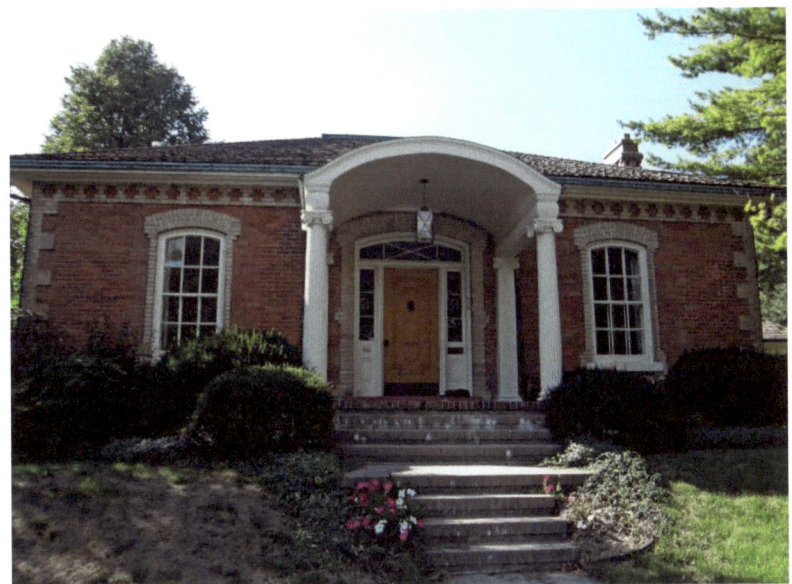

#46 – dichromatic brickwork, corner quoins, arched window voussoirs, pillars with scroll-like capitals

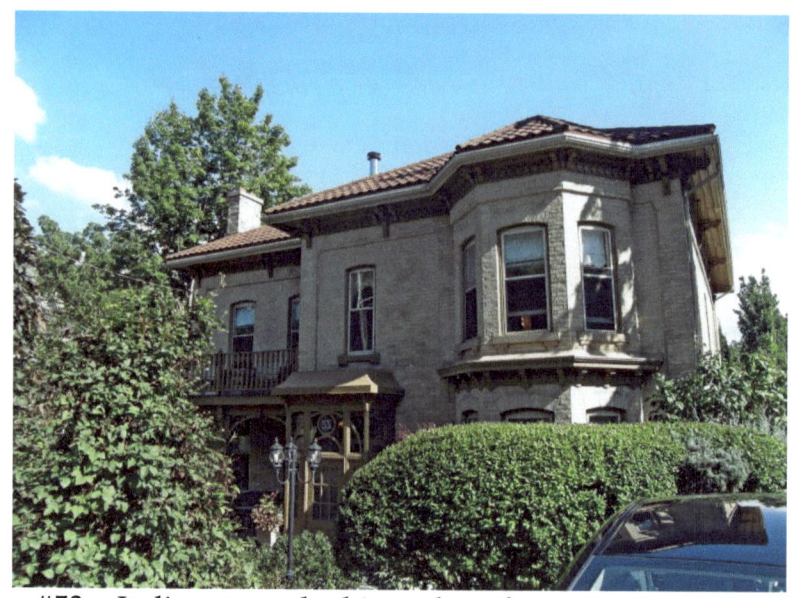

#53 – Italianate style, hipped roof, cornice brackets,
two-storey bay window

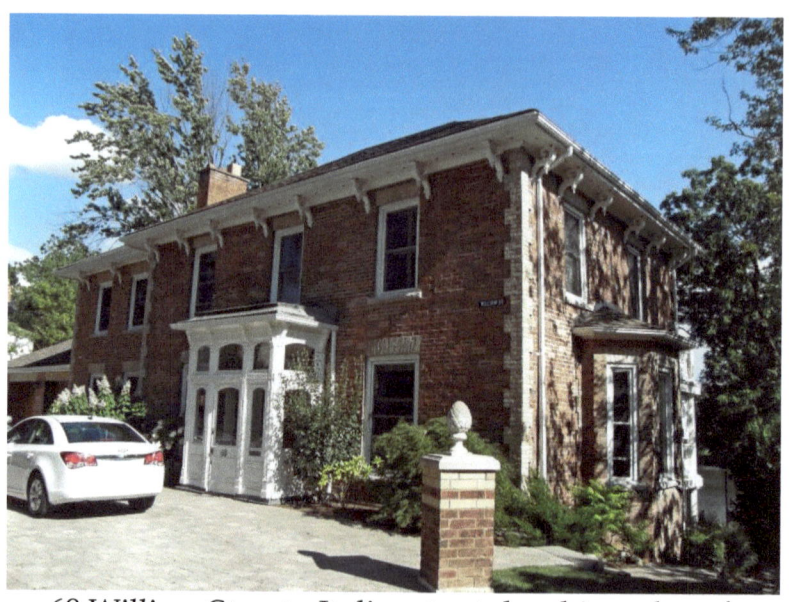

69 William Street - Italianate style – hipped roof,
cornice brackets, corner quoins

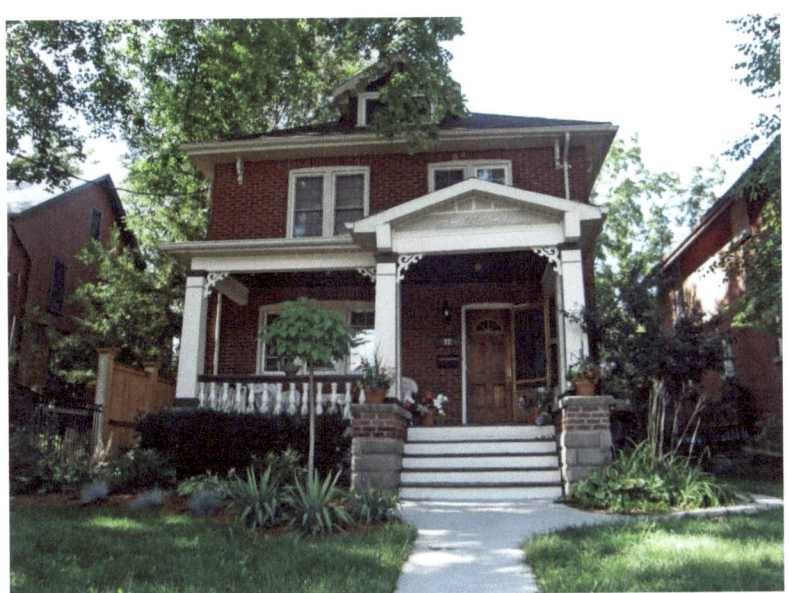

72 Mornington Street - Italianate – dormer in the attic

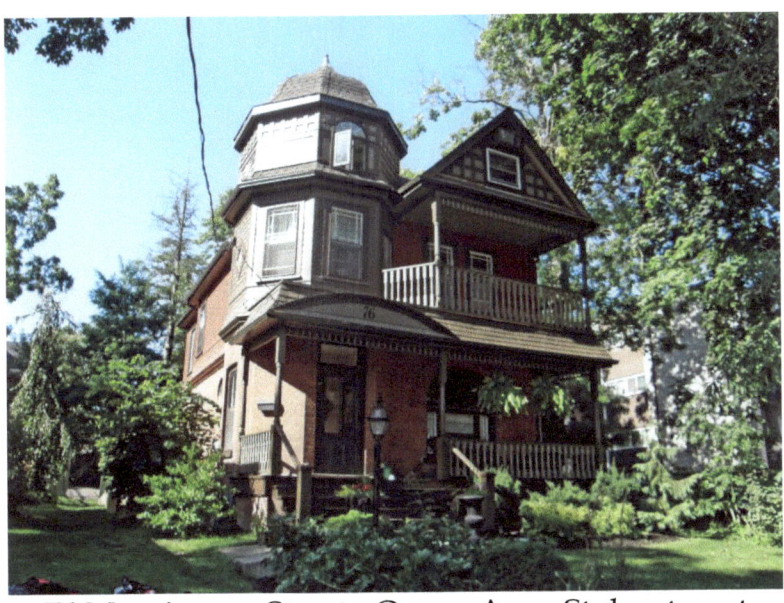

76 Mornington Street - Queen Anne Style – turret

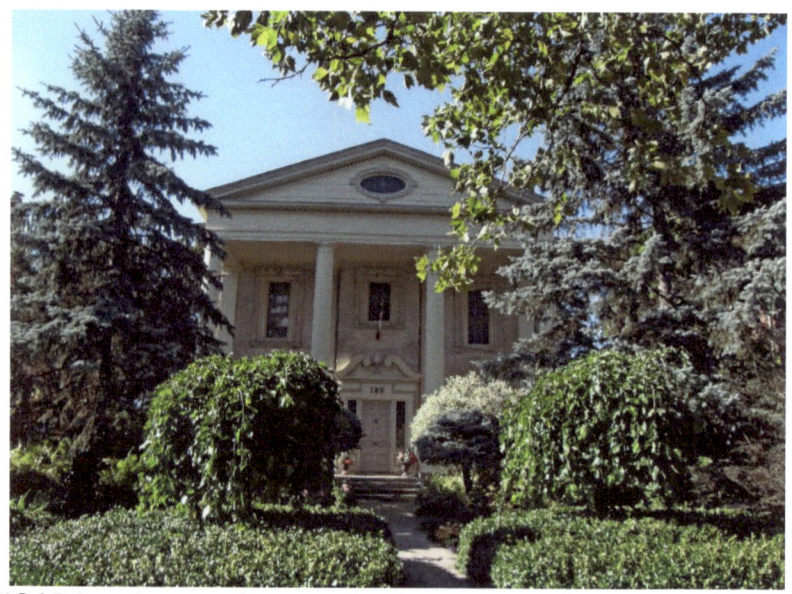

186 Mornington Street – Italianate – pediment with oval window in tympanum

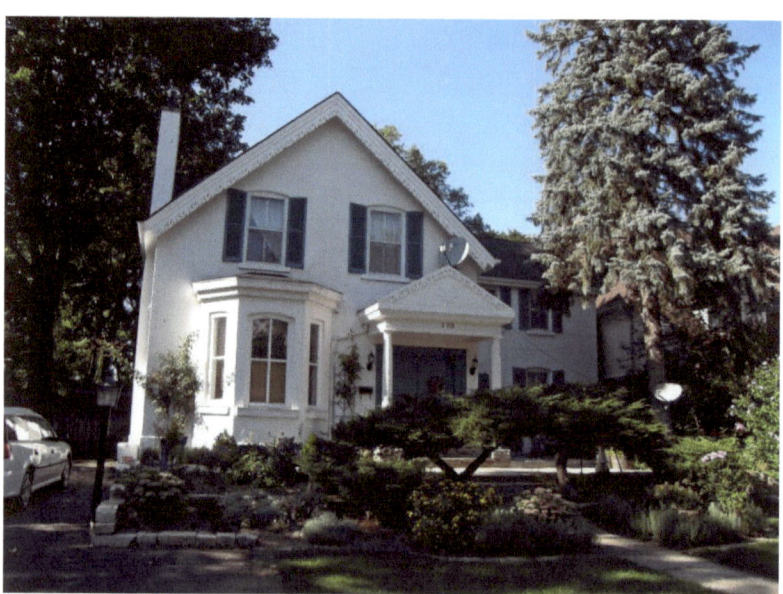

170 Mornington Street - Gothic Revival, bay window

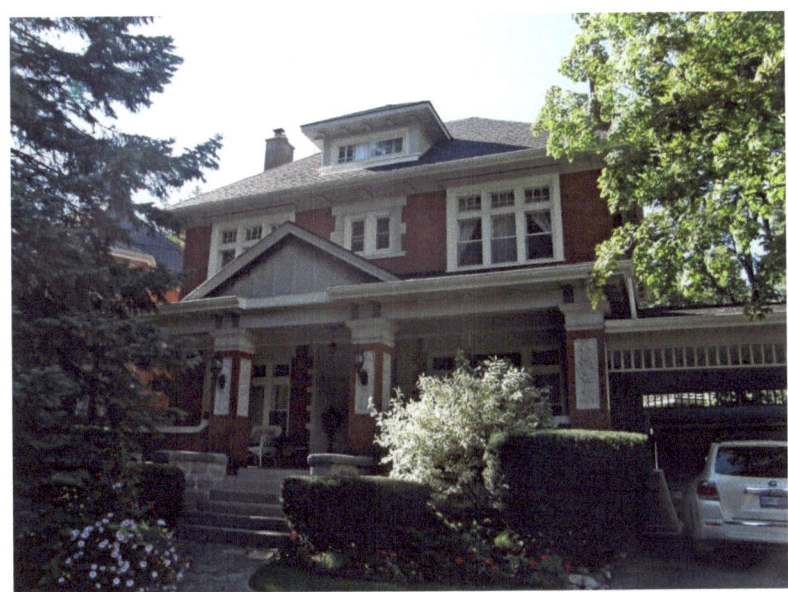

160 Mornington Street – Italianate, pediment, dormer in attic

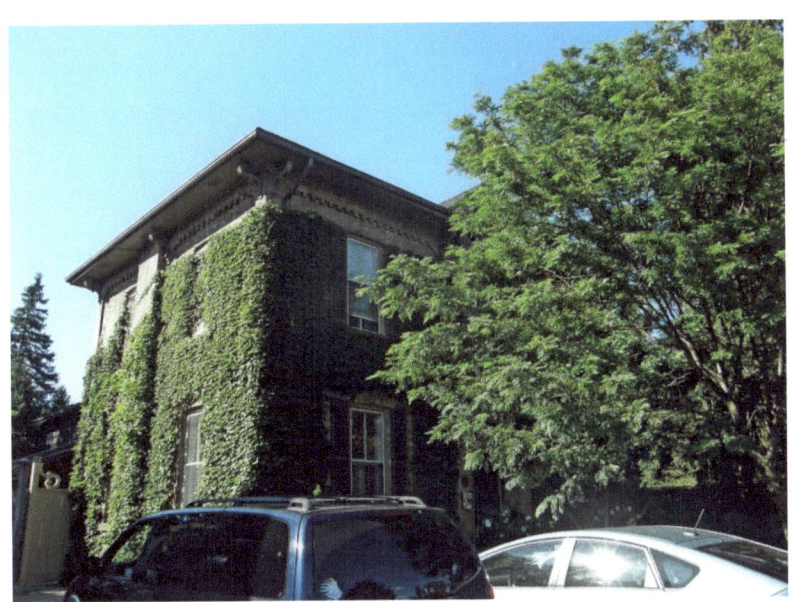

126 Mornington Street – heritage property – Italianate style built in 1879 – former residence of Major James Cardwell Makins (WWI) who became a Justice of the Supreme Court of Ontario in 1934

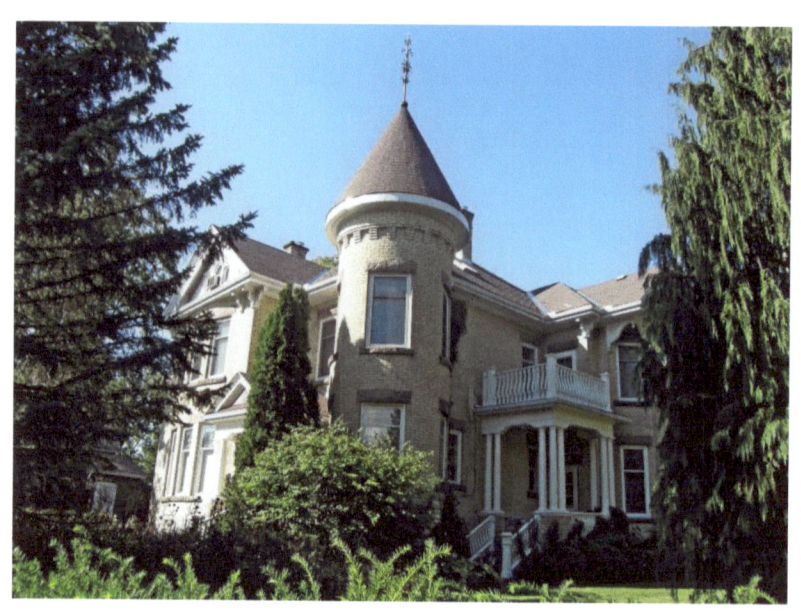

2 Britannia Street - Queen Anne style
– turret with cone-shaped cap

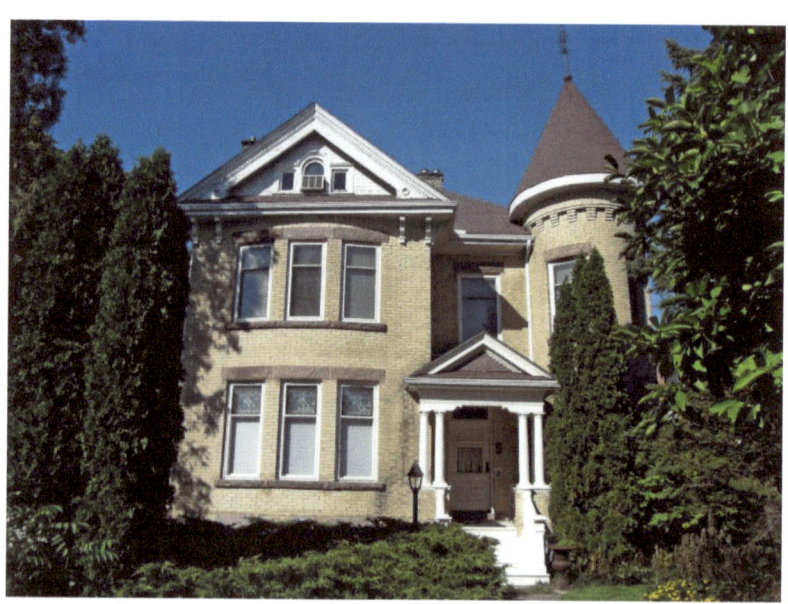

Palladian window in gable, cornice brackets

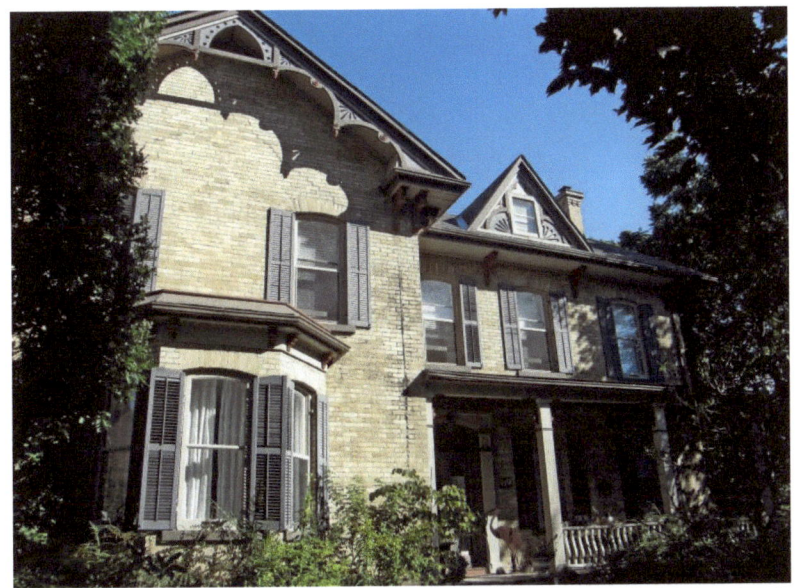

119 Mornington Street – Gothic Revival, Vergeboard trim

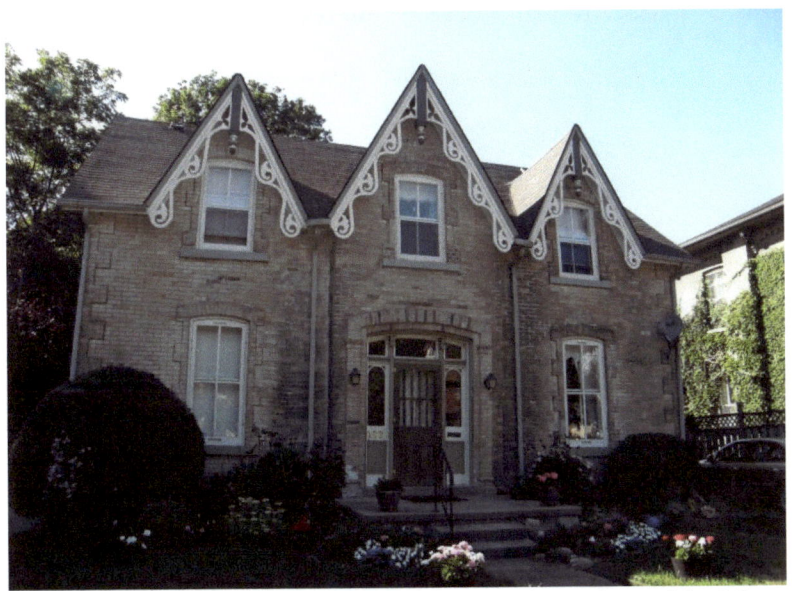

122 Mornington Street – Gothic Revival triple-gabled home, Vergeboard trim on gables, finials, corner quoins; front door has bracketed transom and sidelight windows

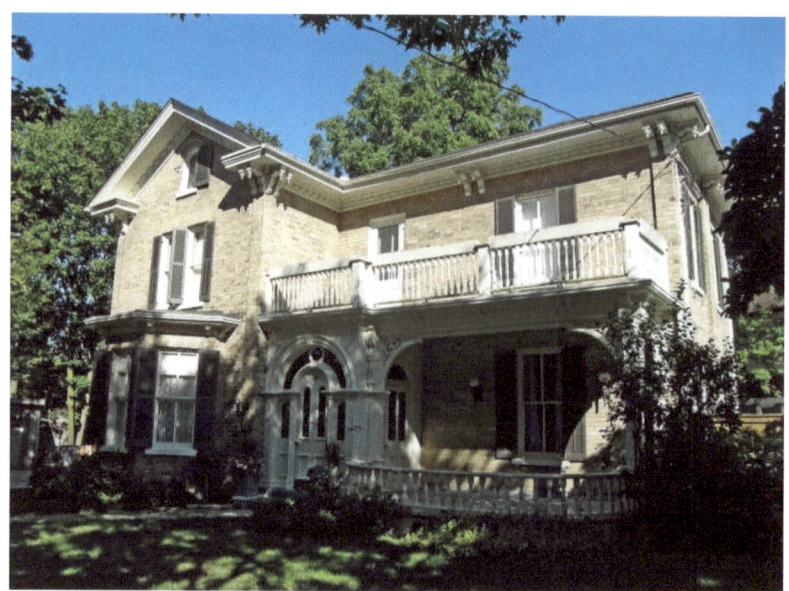

109 Mornington Street – Italianate with two-and-a-half storey tower-like frontispiece with bay window on ground floor, second floor balcony, cornice return on gable, paired cornice brackets

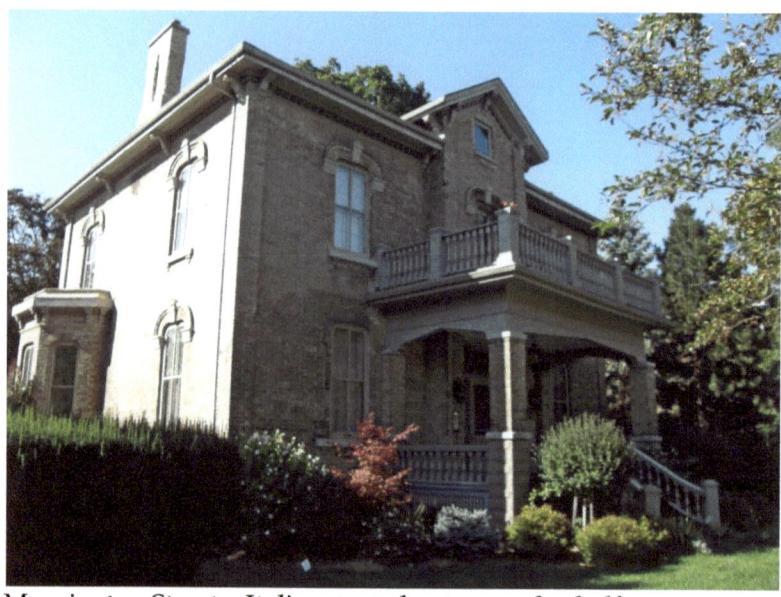

108 Mornington Street – Italianate style - two-and-a-half storey tower-like frontispiece, window voussoirs and keystones

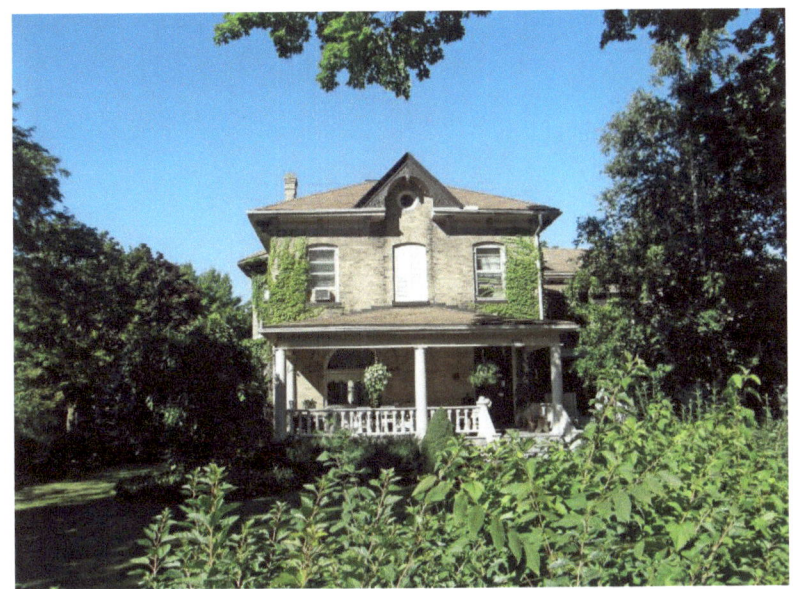

12-14-16 Elizabeth Street – Italianate, built of yellow brick in 1882 – bargeboard trim on gable – heritage property

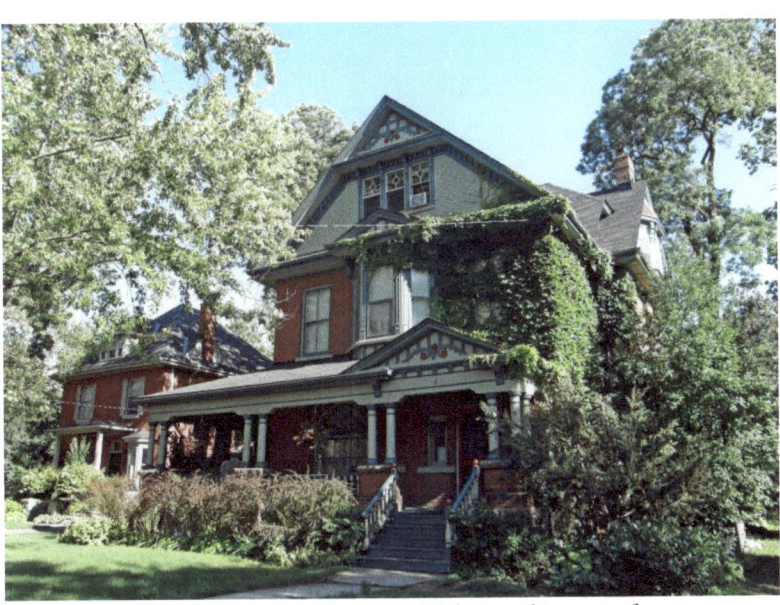

5 Caledonia Street – Edwardian style

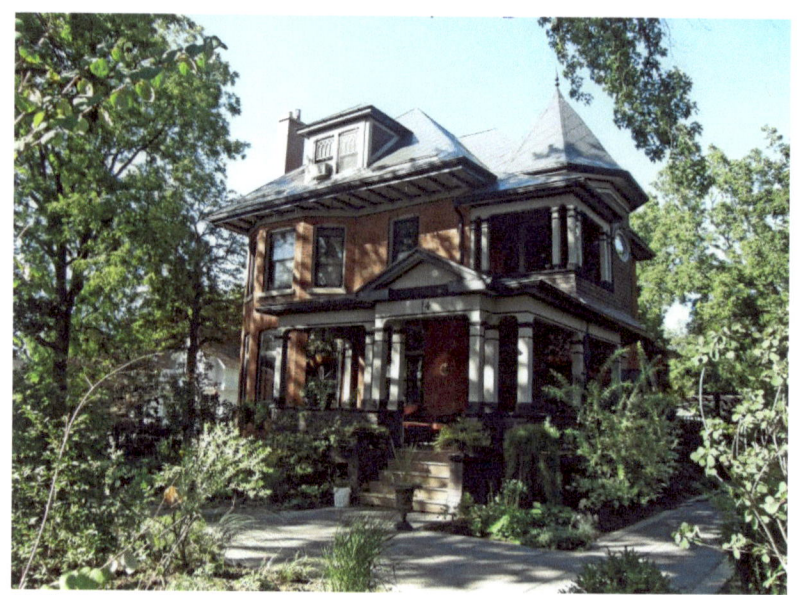

14 Caledonia Street – Queen Anne Revival style built in 1905
– Heritage property

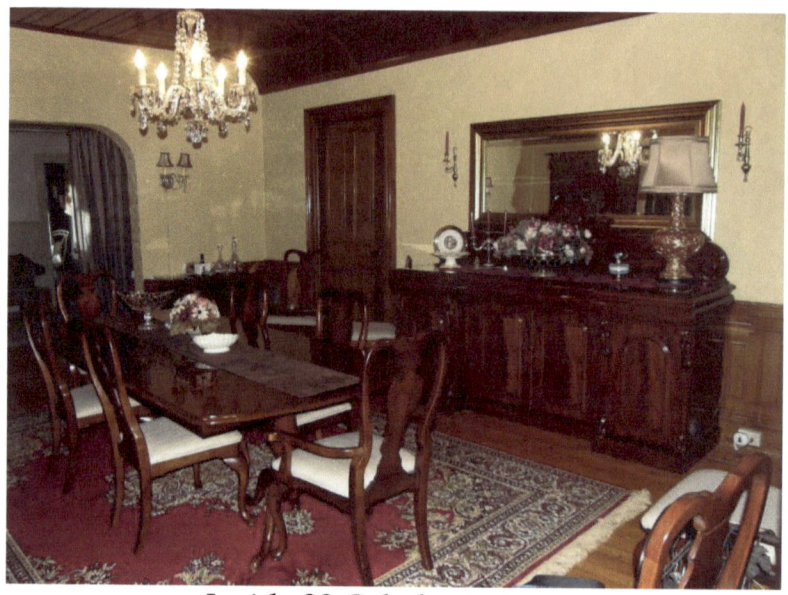

Inside 20 Caledonia Street

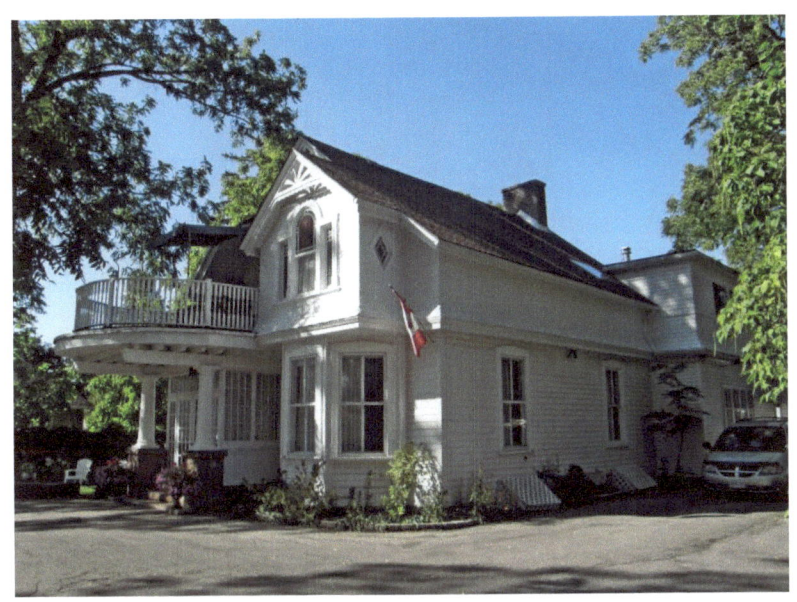

20 Caledonia Street

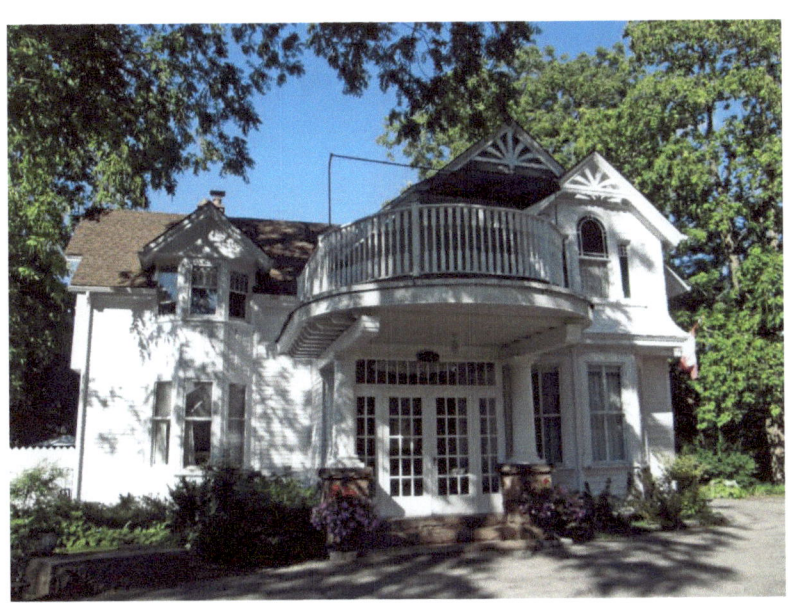

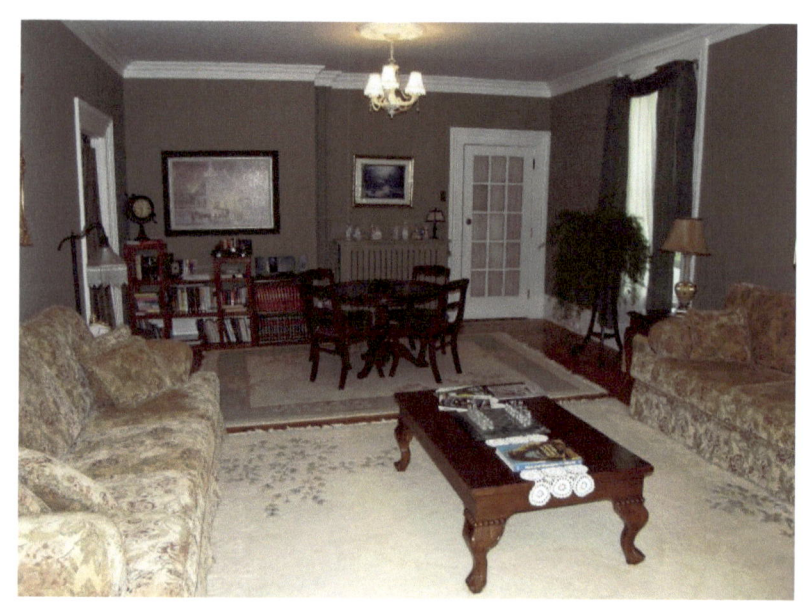

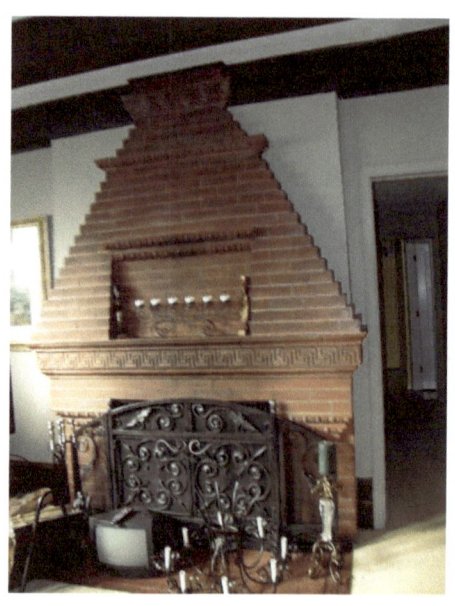

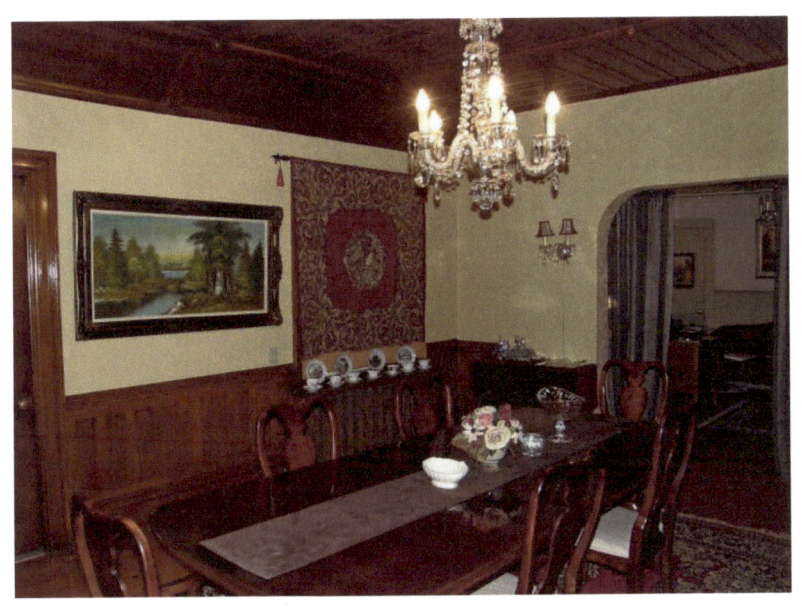

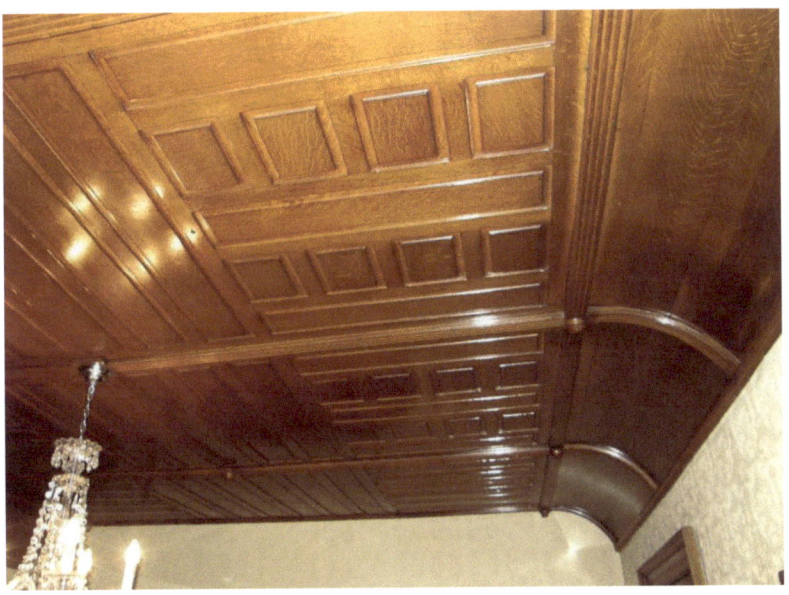

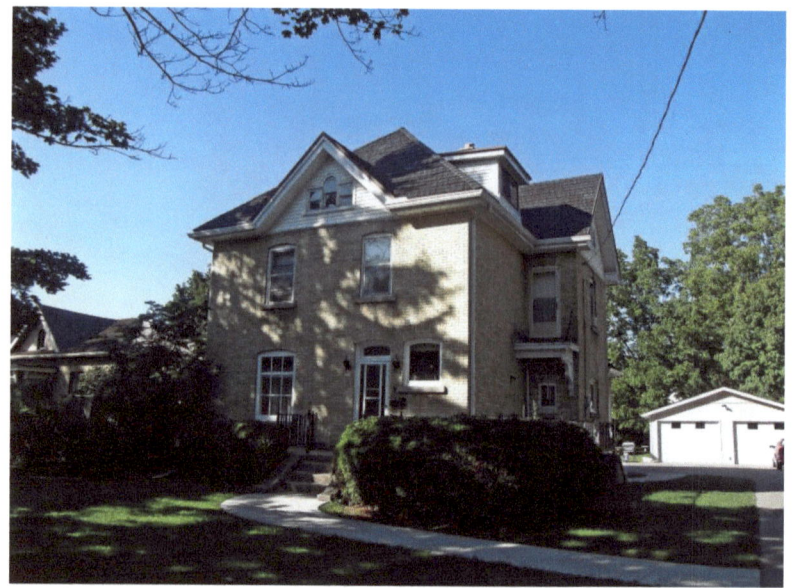

Italianate with two-and-a-half storey tower-like bay,
Palladian window in gable, dormer in attic

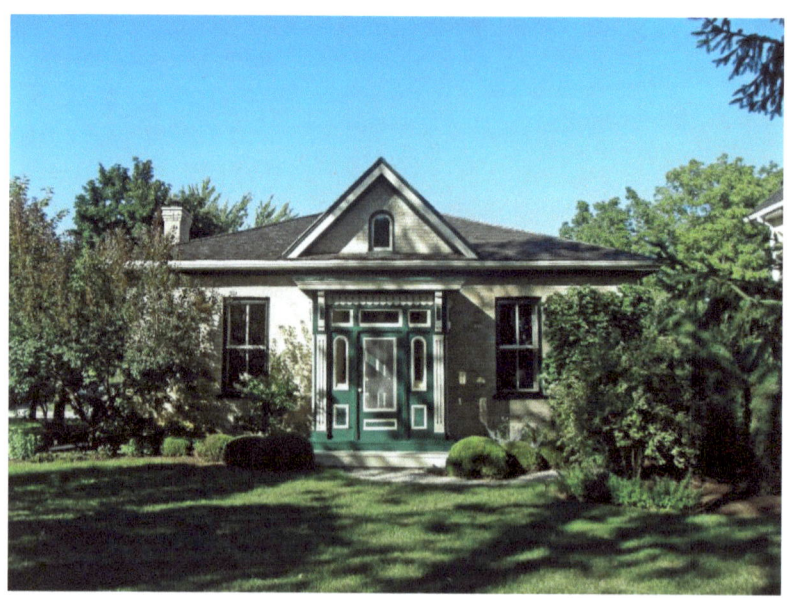

Regency Cottage

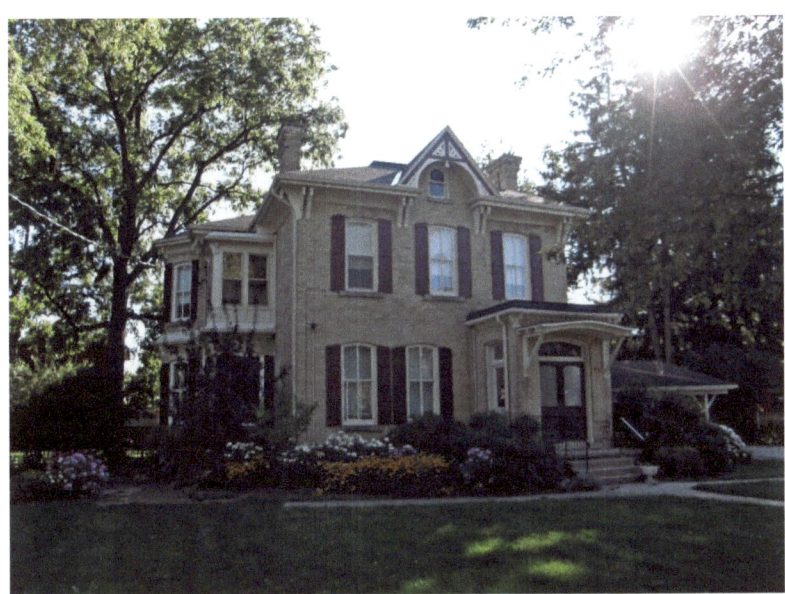

Italianate – Vergeboard trim on gable, paired cornice brackets, two-storey bay windows on side

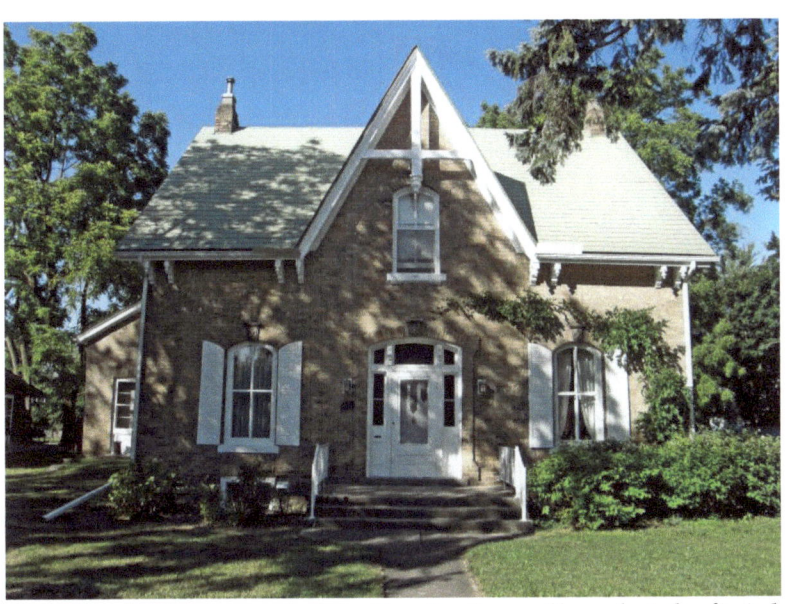

67 Caledonia Street - Gothic Revival – yellow brick, finial on gable, paired cornice brackets, window voussoirs and keystones

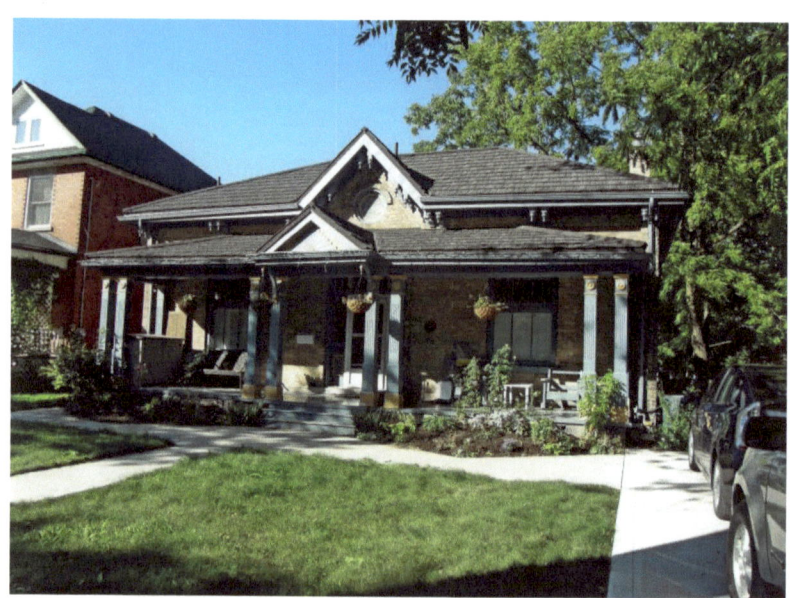

68 Caledonia Street – Regency Cottage - built in 1876 – Ontario cottage gable – original decorative brick and woodwork

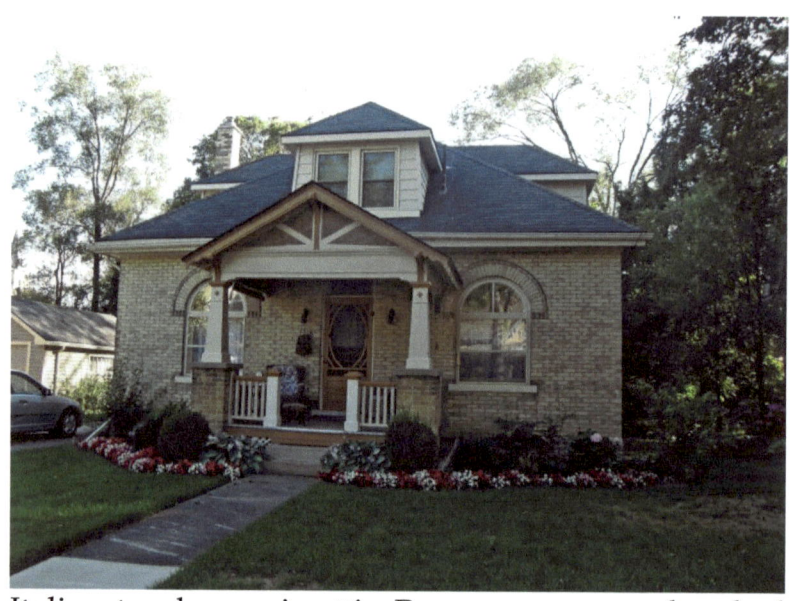

Italianate –dormer in attic, Romanesque round-arched window voussoirs

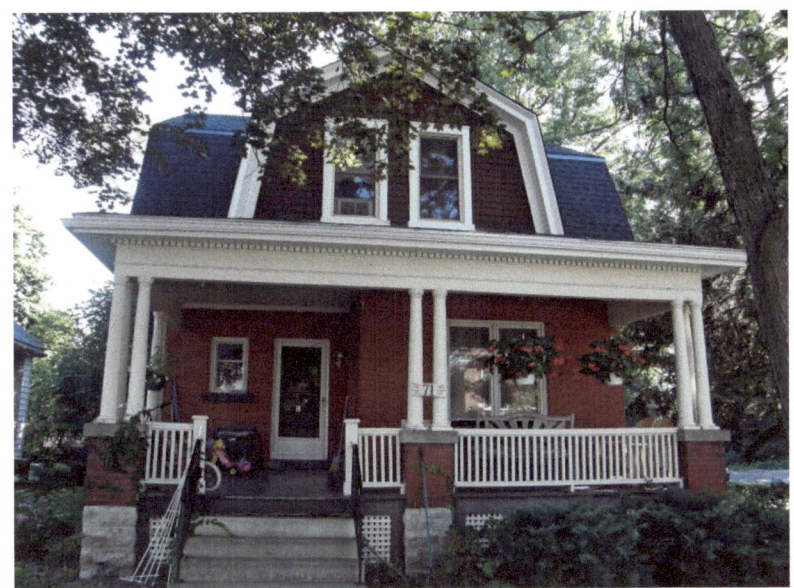

71 Caledonia Street

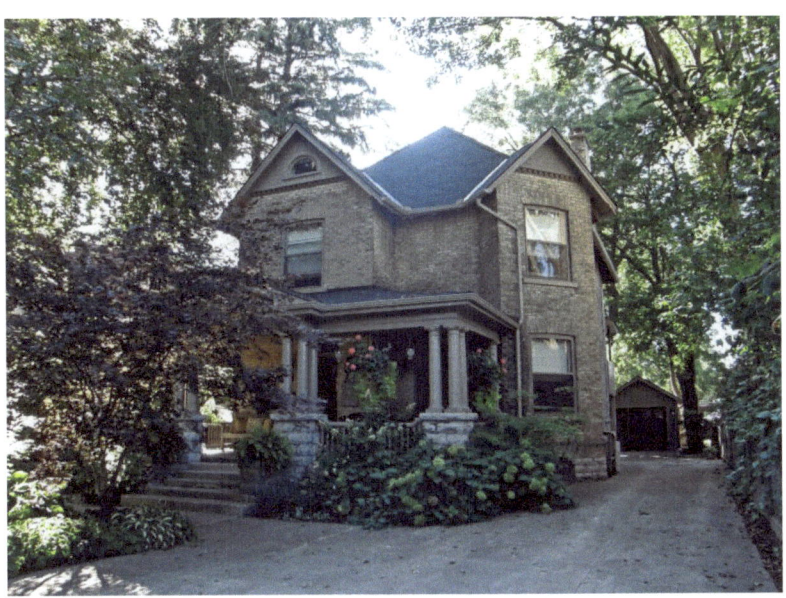

Italianate – dentil moulding

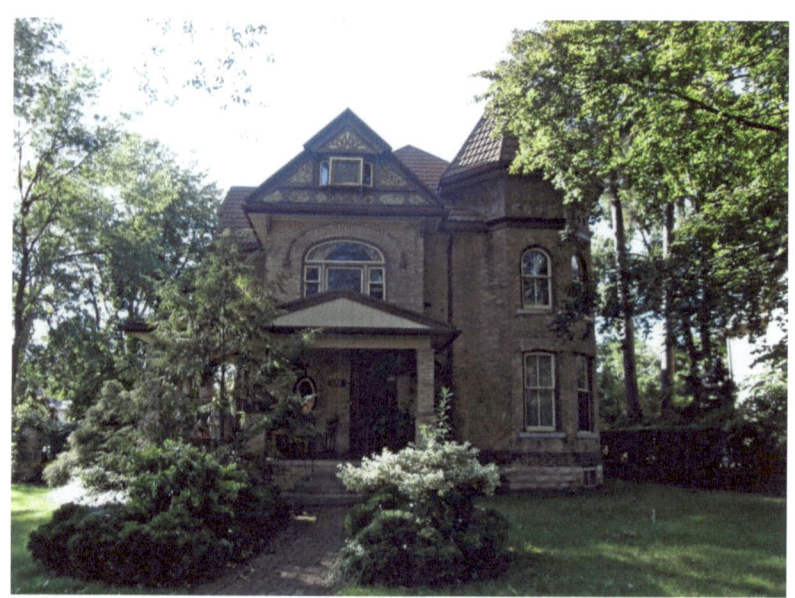

120 Caledonia Street – Queen Anne style
Romanesque round-arched window voussoirs

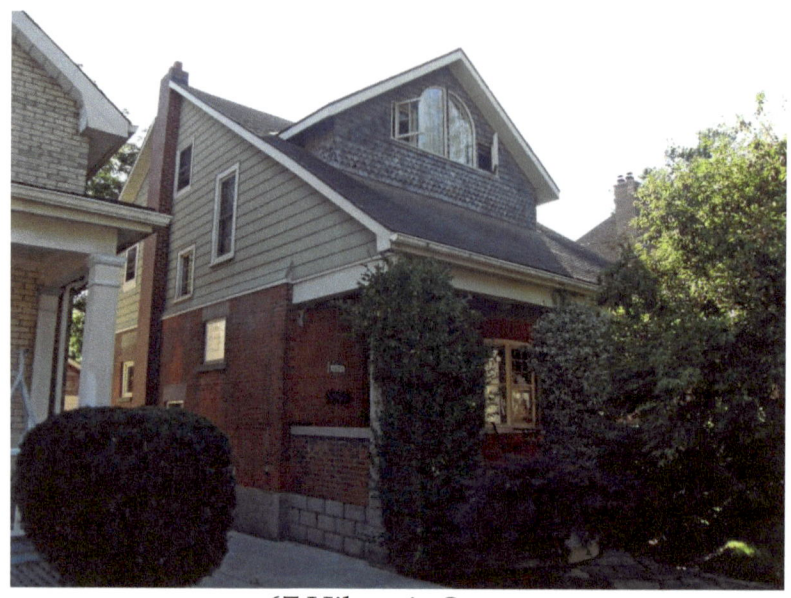

67 Hibernia Street

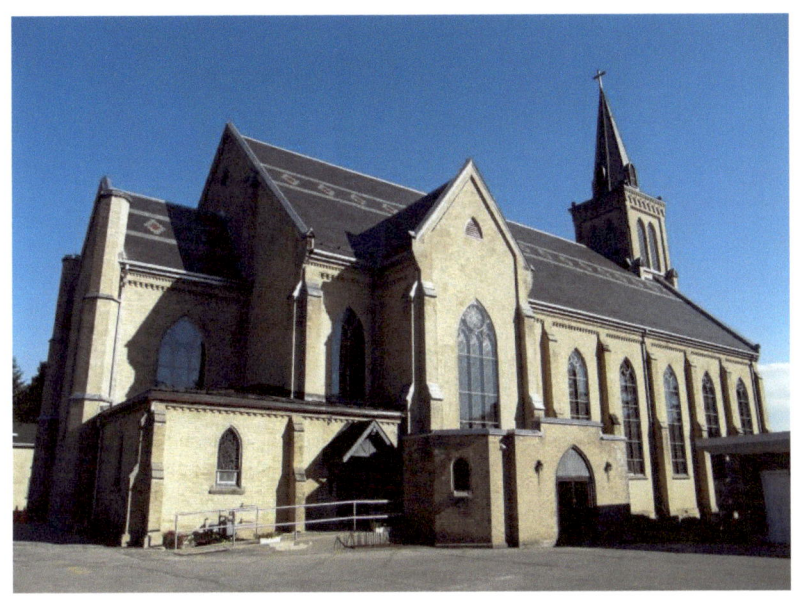

96 Huron Street - St. Joseph's Catholic Church
– dichromatic tile work on roof

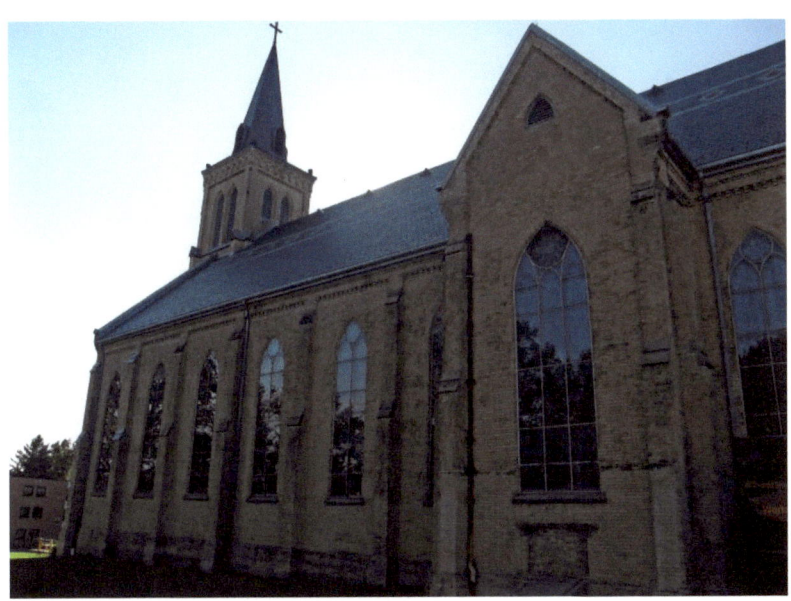

Lancet windows

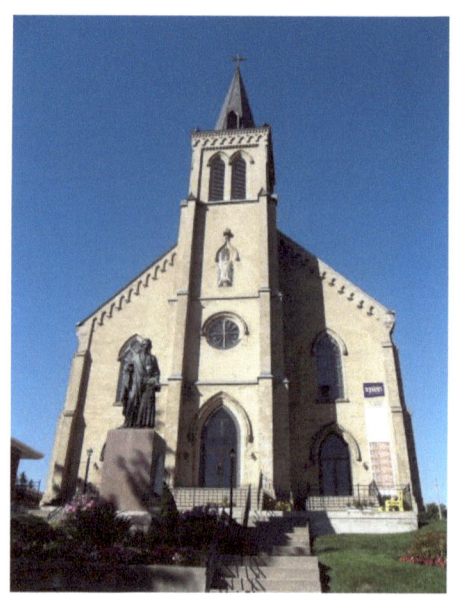

Bell tower

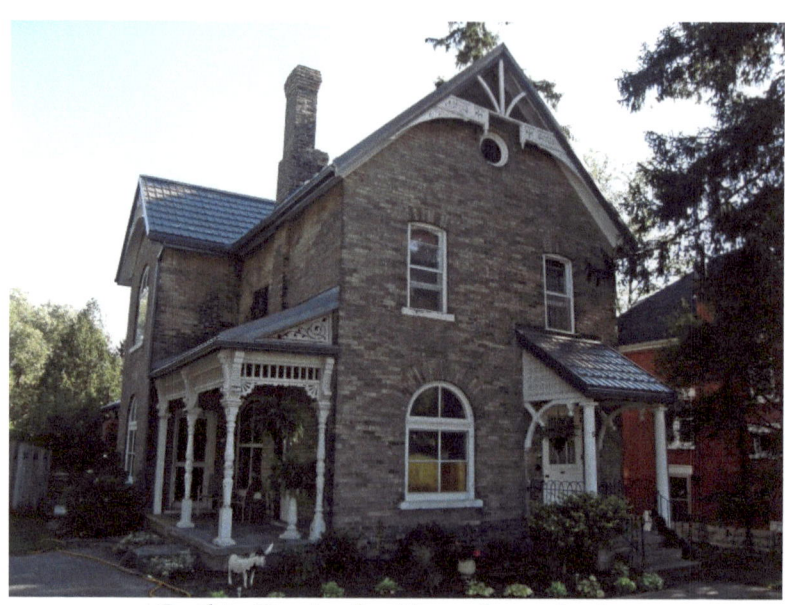

Gothic Revival – Vergeboard trim

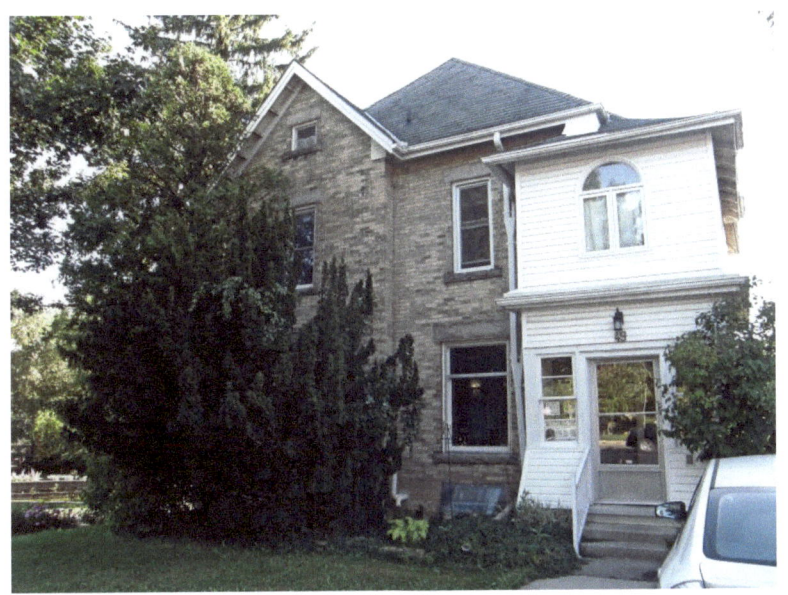

Douglas Street

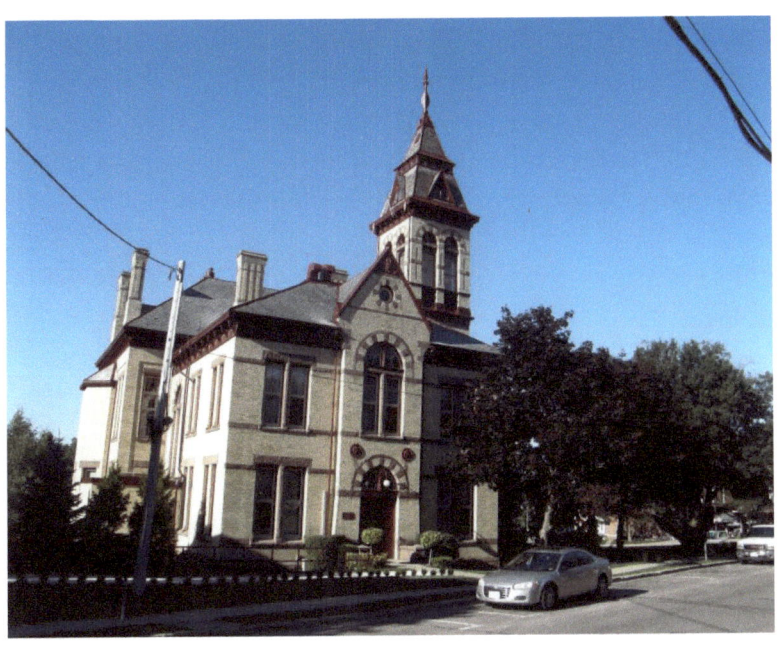

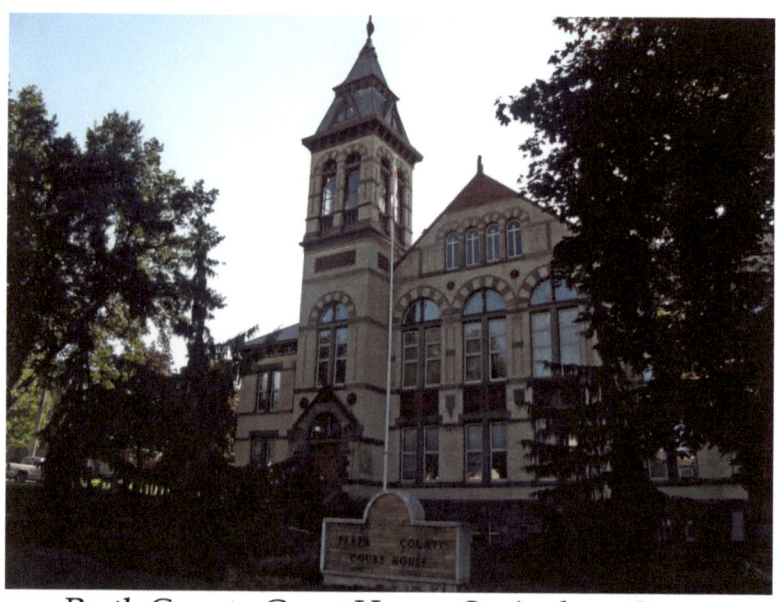

Perth County Court House, St. Andrew Street
– opened May 9, 1887
– High Victorian architecture with terra cotta details

It combines bichromal (multi-coloured) masonry and a variety of building materials with features from different architectural styles. Italianate brackets adorn the cornice, while several Queen Anne features include the medieval tower, moulded brick chimneys, and small multiple paned windows.

Several features of the Romanesque Revival style include the round arch windows stretching over two storeys, the heavy doors, the contrasting masonry surfaces, the rusticated basement foundation, the wall dormers which peak with a gable at the top, the pinnacle placed off centre, Romanesque motifs adorning the soffits, and miniature columns complete with capitals which embellish the arched windows on the front and side facades. The soffits of the cornice immediately above the terra cotta panel are adorned with an intricate rose and maple leaf pattern.

Quarry stone from Acton was used as the foundation in the basement. Sandstone from Credit Valley was used for the front entrance, and slate for the roof.

Above the main entranceway is a semicircular transom, with stained glass windows portraying the scales of justice and crossed swords. Two panels with hands giving benediction are also located here. Quoins are used to create a pilaster effect complete with capitals on either side of the entrance, giving a bichromal contrast against the buff-coloured brick.

To the right of the tower are six allegorical terra cotta panels representing:
1. Arts: angels with musical instruments, a score, and painter's brushes represent the arts.
2. Manufacture: measuring instruments and gears symbolize manufacturing.
3 & 4. Justice: a sword surmounted by a lion's head and a set of scales represent justice and the role of the building as a court house.
5. Agriculture: a sheaf of wheat, a plough and fruit represent agriculture which has always been the mainstay of the County.
6. Architecture: a compass and other measuring instruments represent architecture, an important element in this building.

Two blank sandstone shields separate these terra cotta panels into pairs. A third blank shield appears on the small tower.

Above the panels are two terra cotta heads representing manufacture and agriculture. At the top, the wall dormer peaks into a gable featuring a terra cotta pediment depicting a female allegory of justice. A lion holding a shield with the initials "PC" for Perth County stands at the top and centre of the facade.

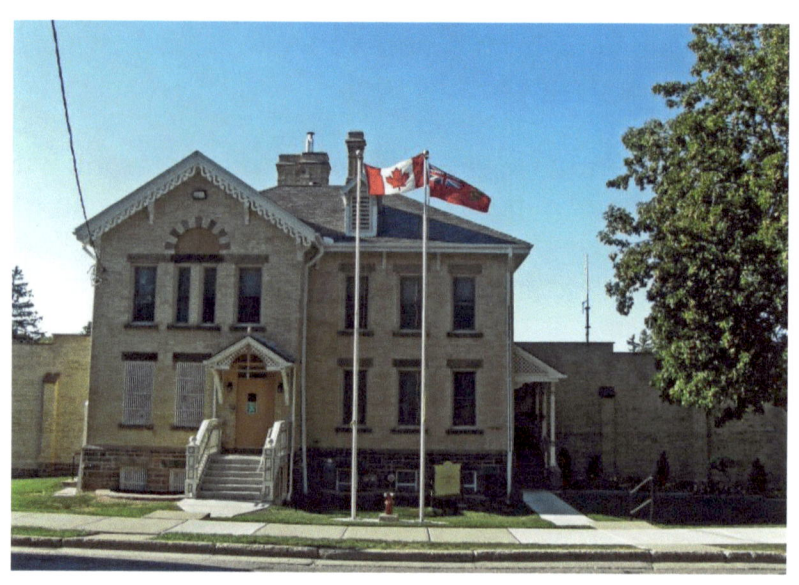

30 St. Andrew Street - Stratford Jail – built in 1886

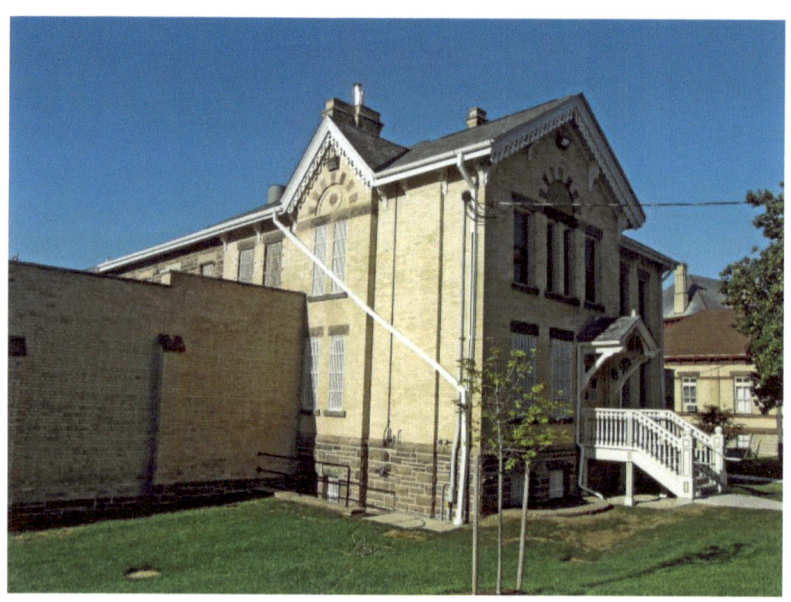

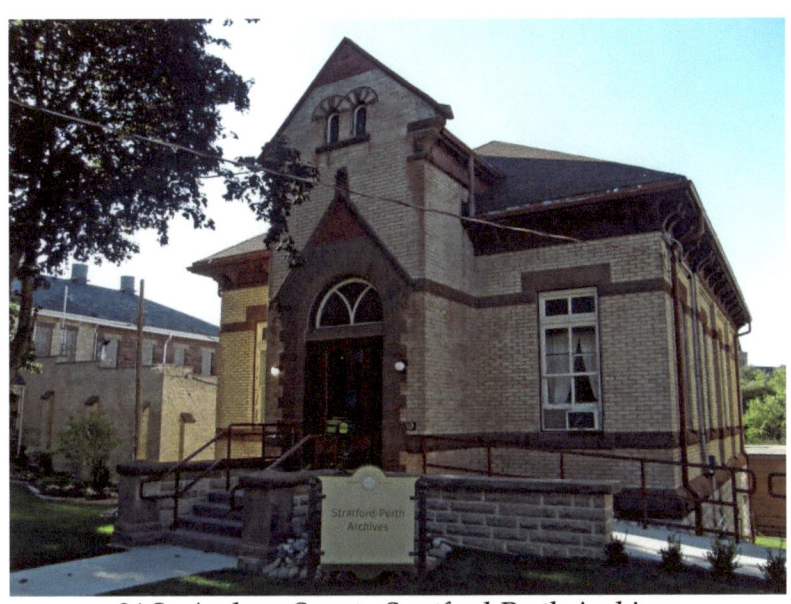

24 St. Andrew Street - Stratford-Perth Archives
– Italianate – dichromatic brickwork - erected in 1910
Quoins are used to create a pilaster effect complete with capitals on either
side of the entrance.

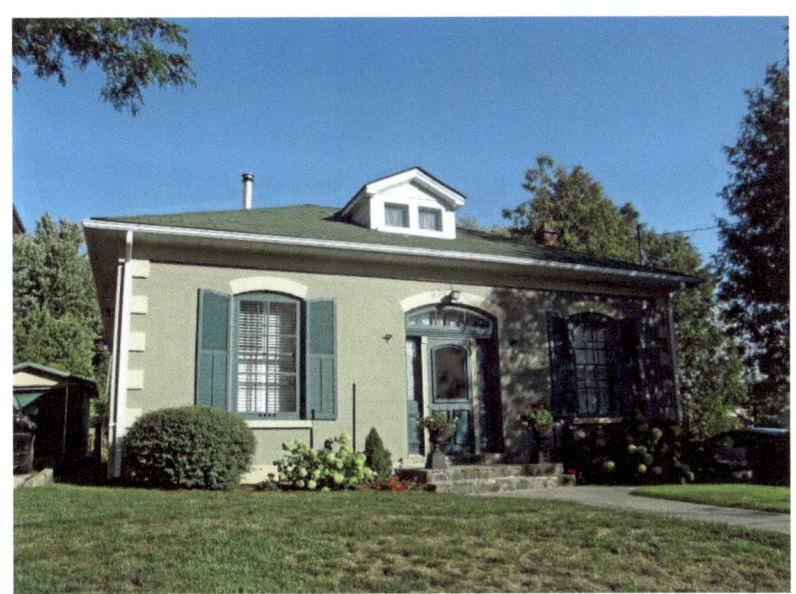

21 St. Andrew Street - Regency Cottage – dormer in attic,
corner quoins

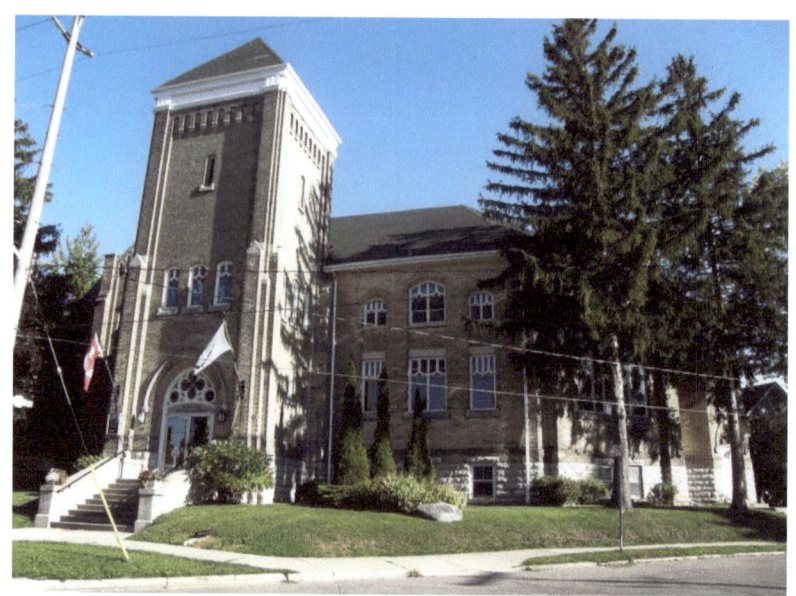

25 St. Andrew Street - St. Andrew's Presbyterian Church
– founded in 1838, rebuilt in 1868 and 1911

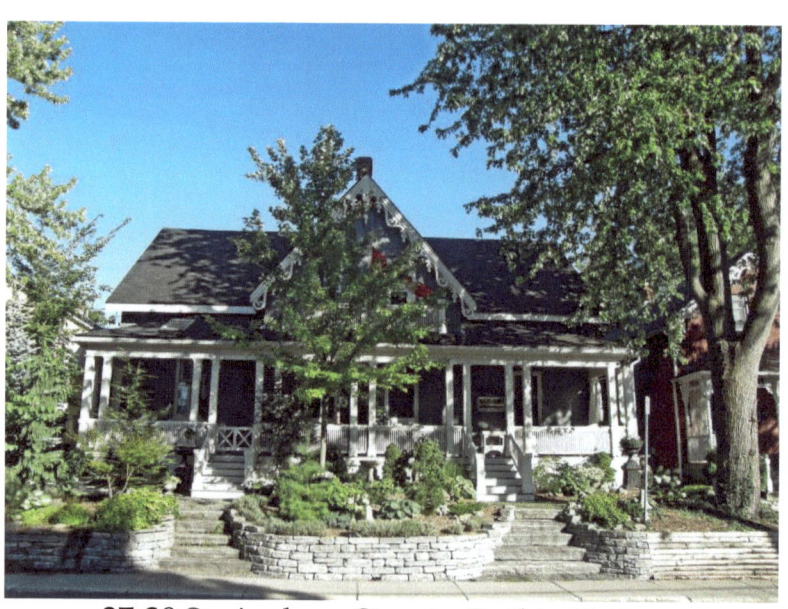

27-29 St. Andrew Street - Gothic Cottage
– Vergeboard trim on gable

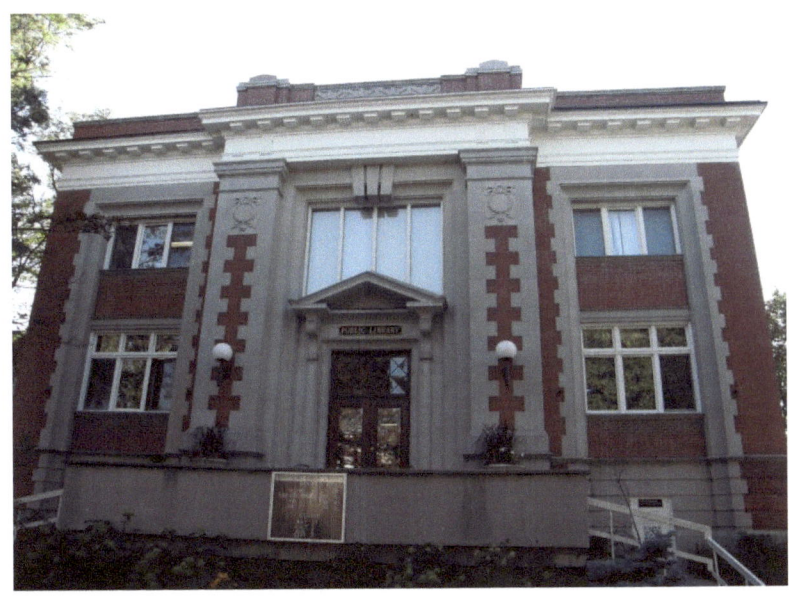

19 St. Andrew Street - Carnegie Public Library built in 1903
Neo-Classical features – tall columns the height of the
building, triangular pediment

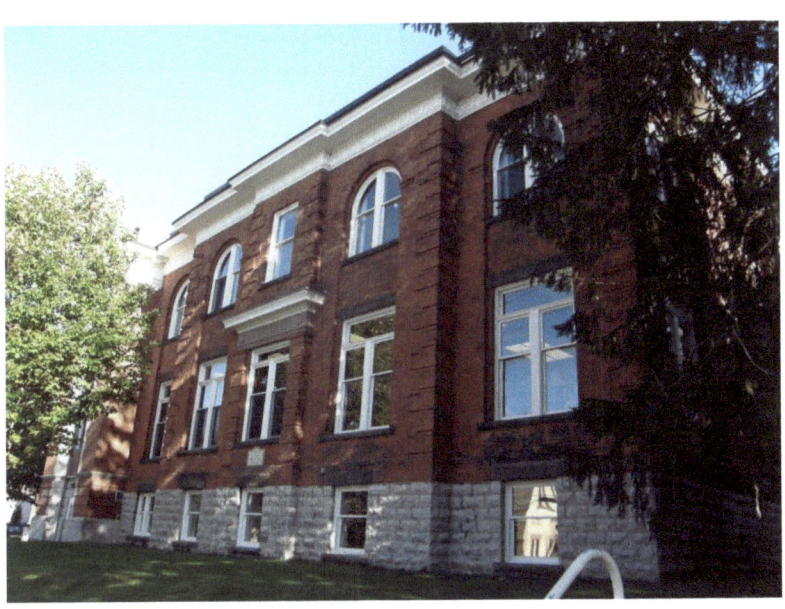

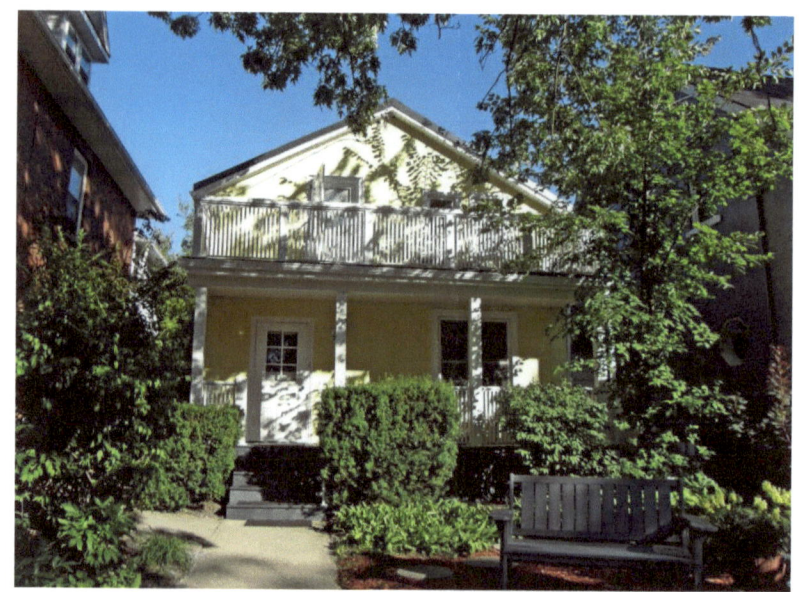

25 St. Andrew Street – Gothic Revival

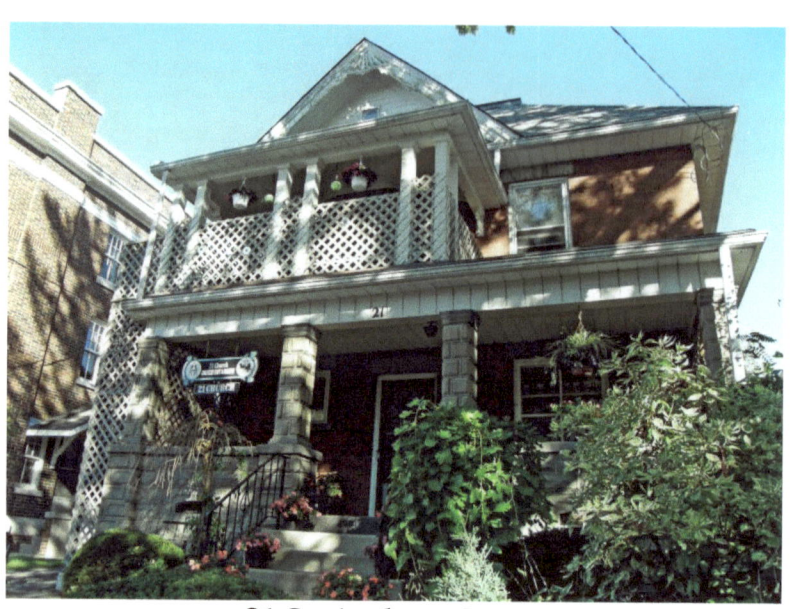

21 St. Andrew Street

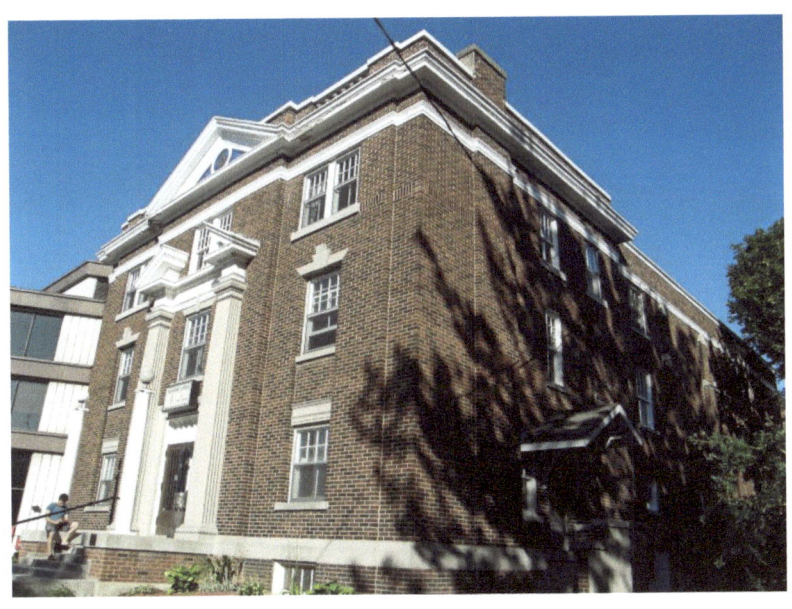

15 Church Street – Masonic Lodge

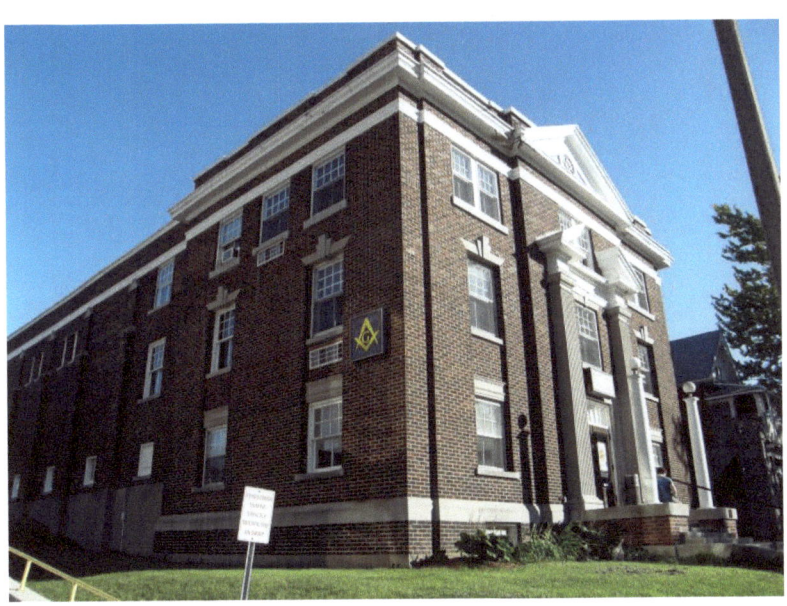

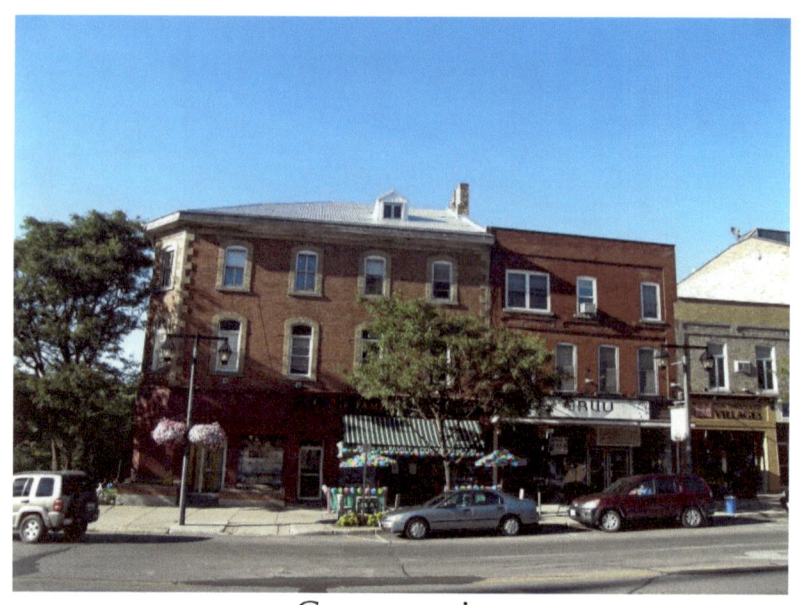

Corner quoins

Ontario Street

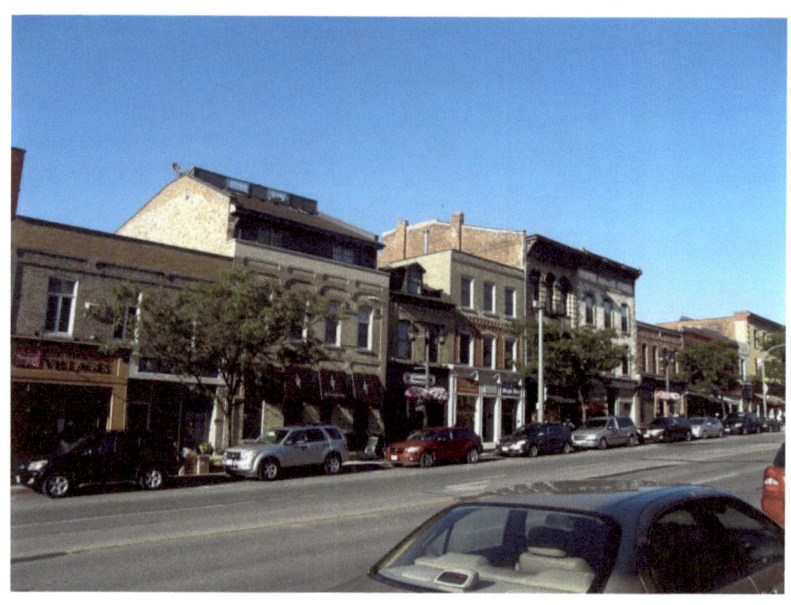

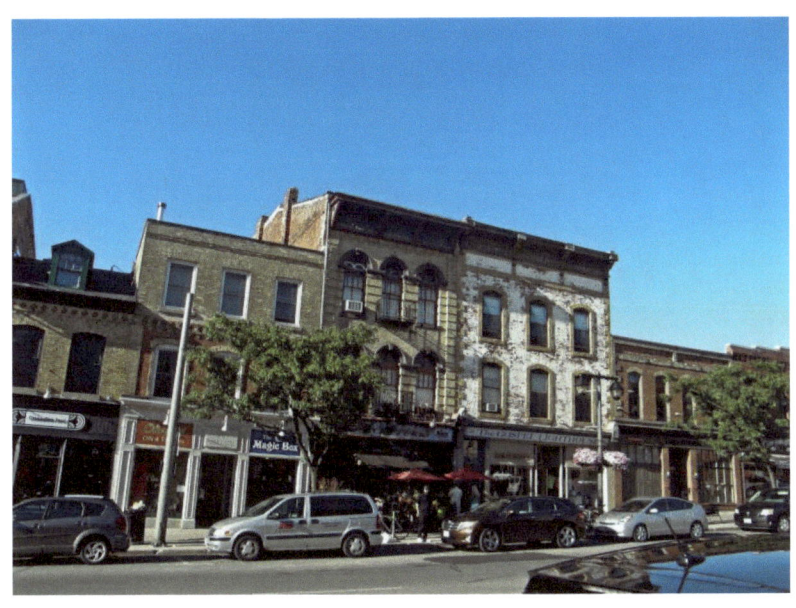

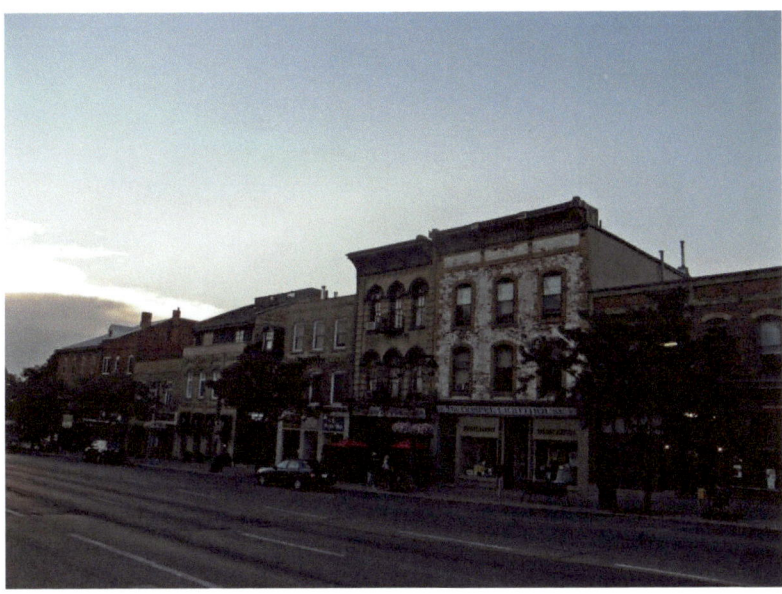

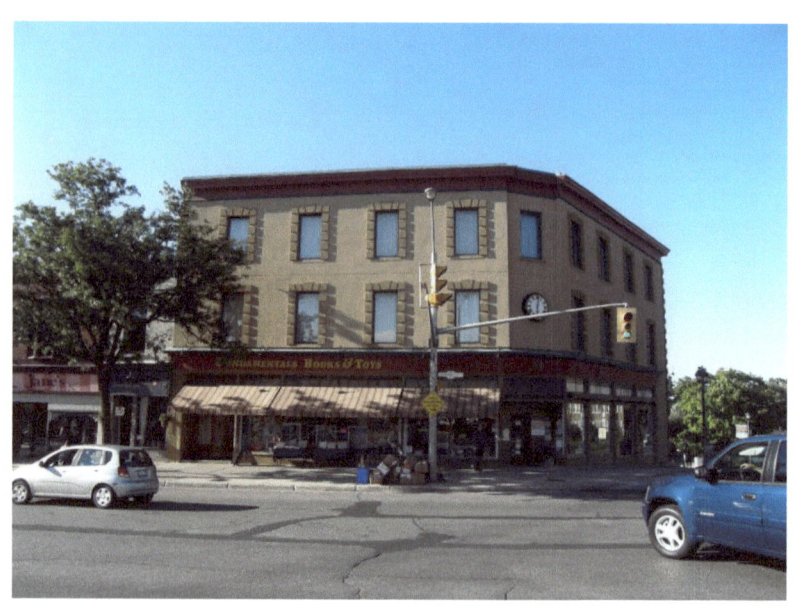

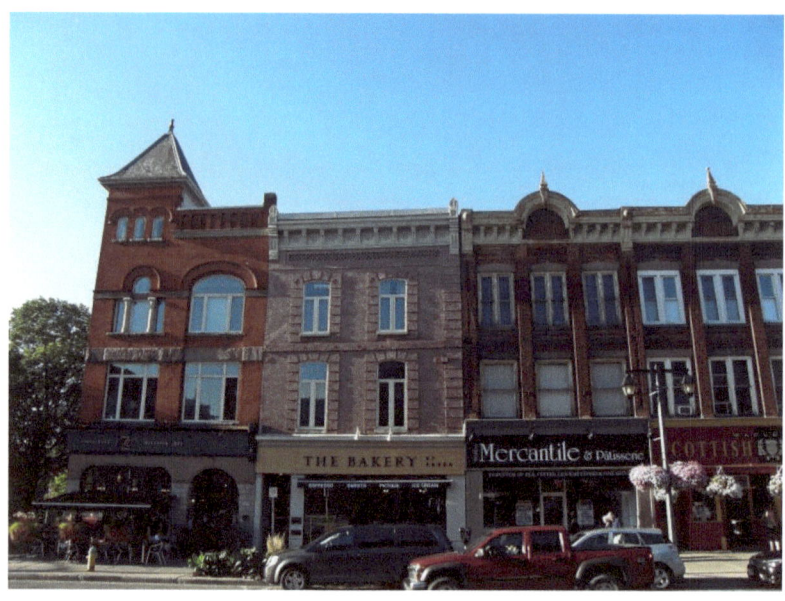

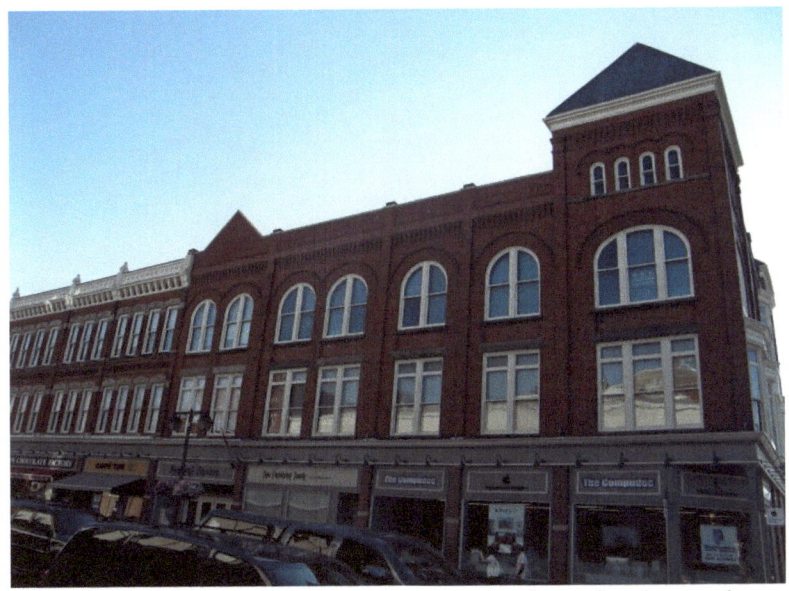

Dentil moulding, Romanesque round-arched windows

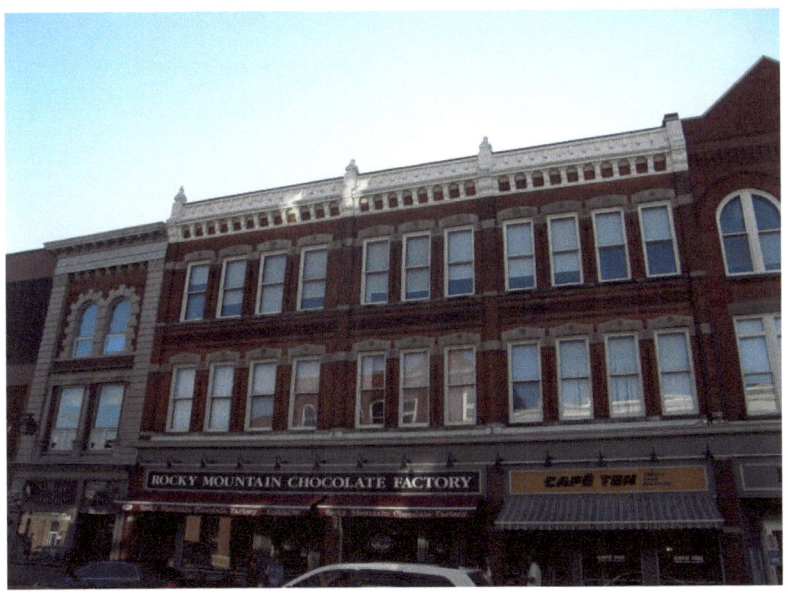

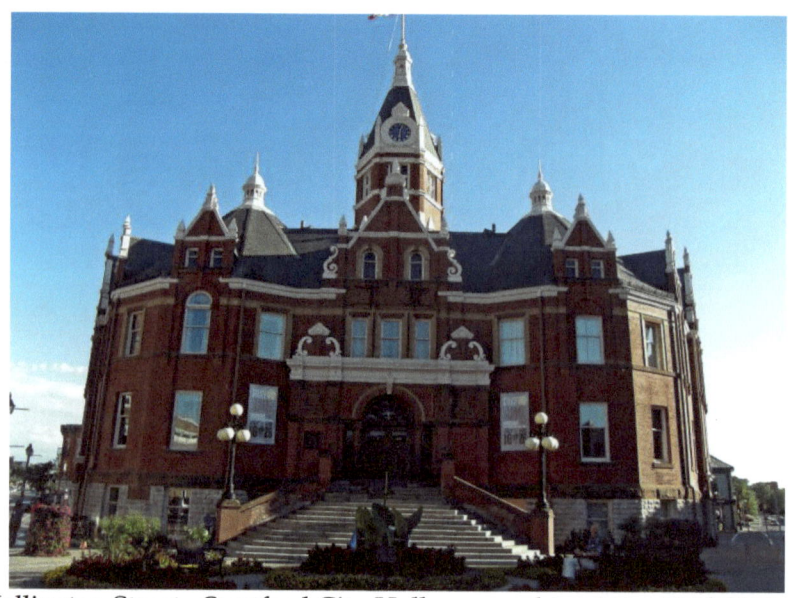

1 Wellington Street - Stratford City Hall – opened in 1900 – High Victorian building with many Queen Anne features – textural and bichromal wall materials, Flemish wall dormers, and Neo-Classical cupolas and arches – geometric building with a dodecagon (twelve-sided shape) on either side of the outside triangular stairwell

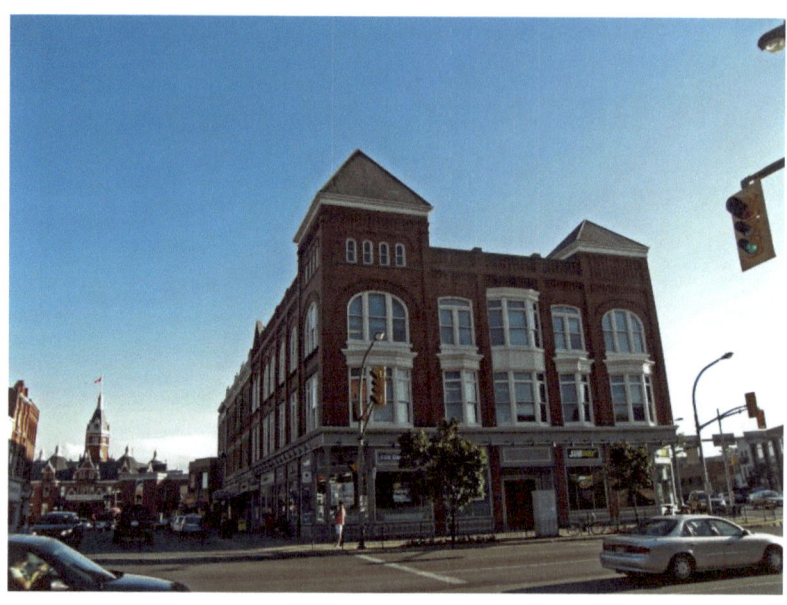

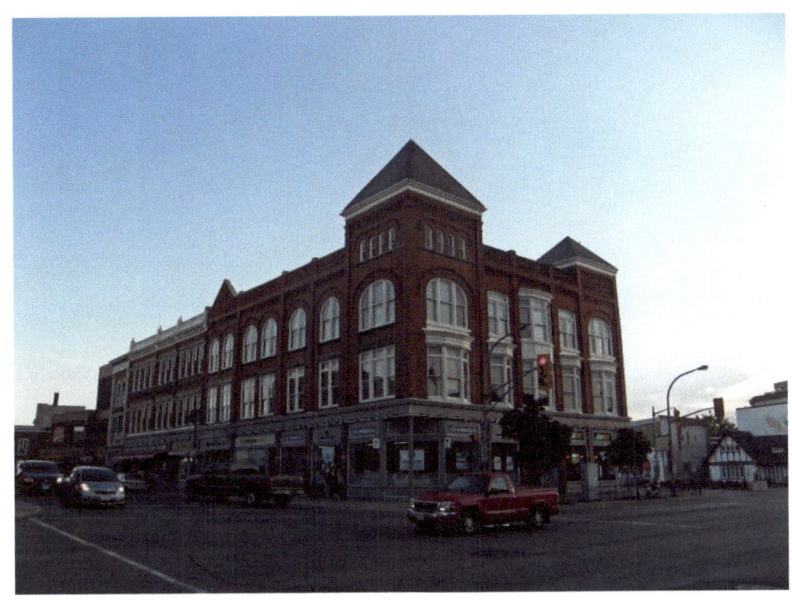

Festival Square

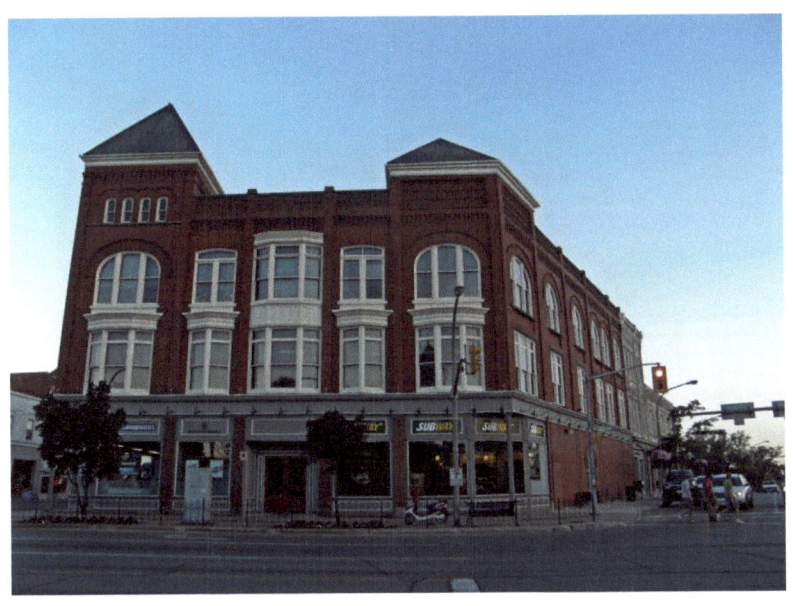

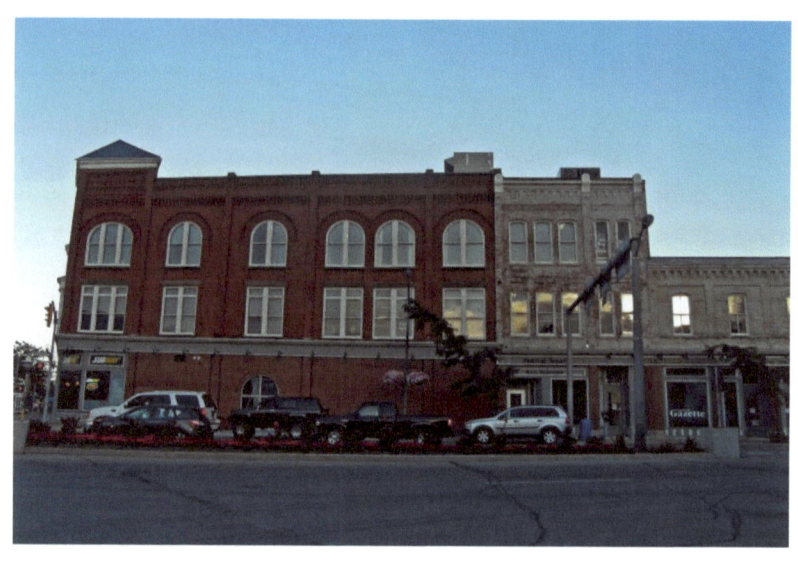

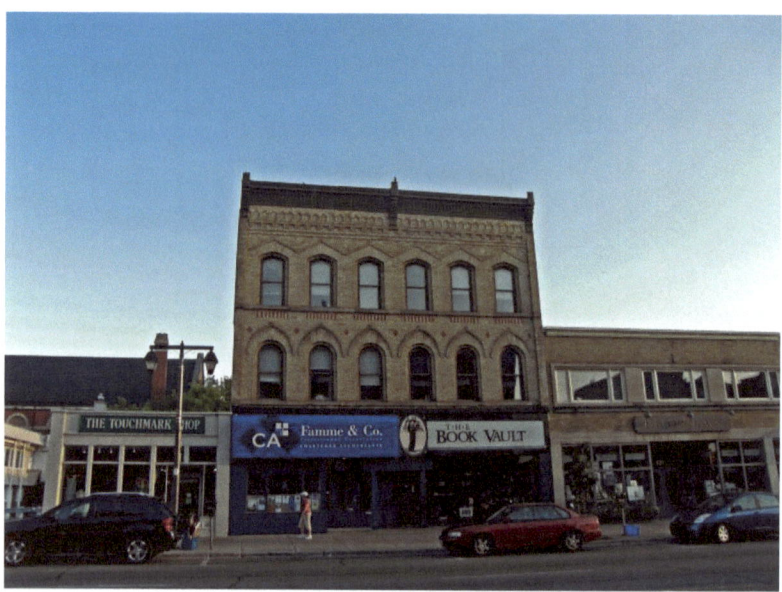

131 Ontario Street – dentil moulding, dichromatic brickwork, arched window voussoirs

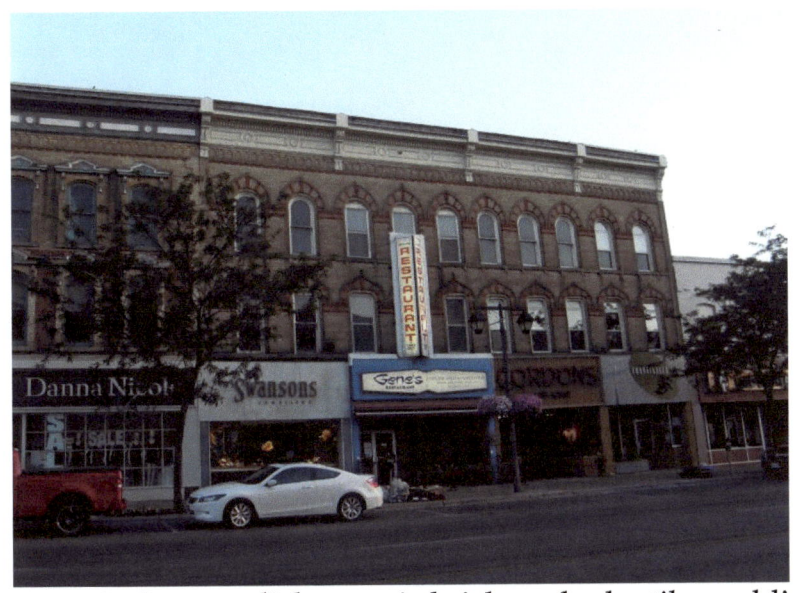

81 Ontario Street – dichromatic brickwork, dentil moulding

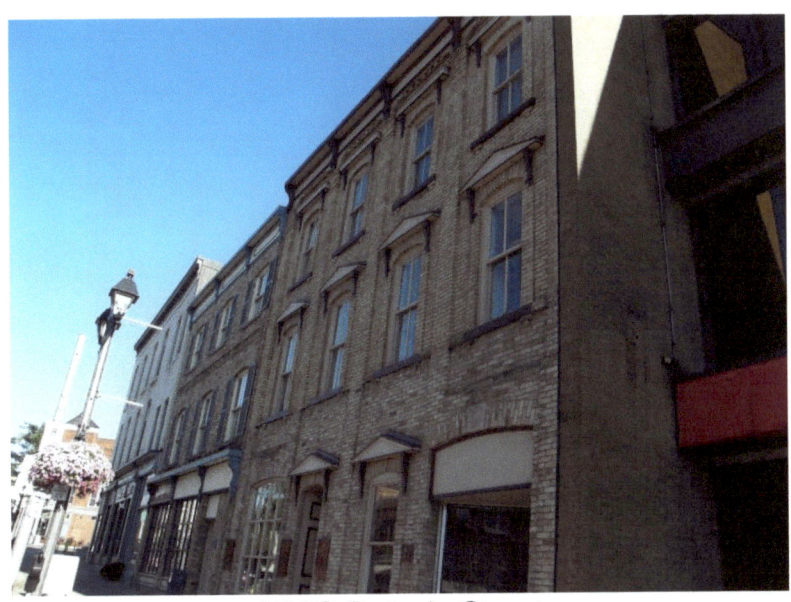

17-19 Ontario Street

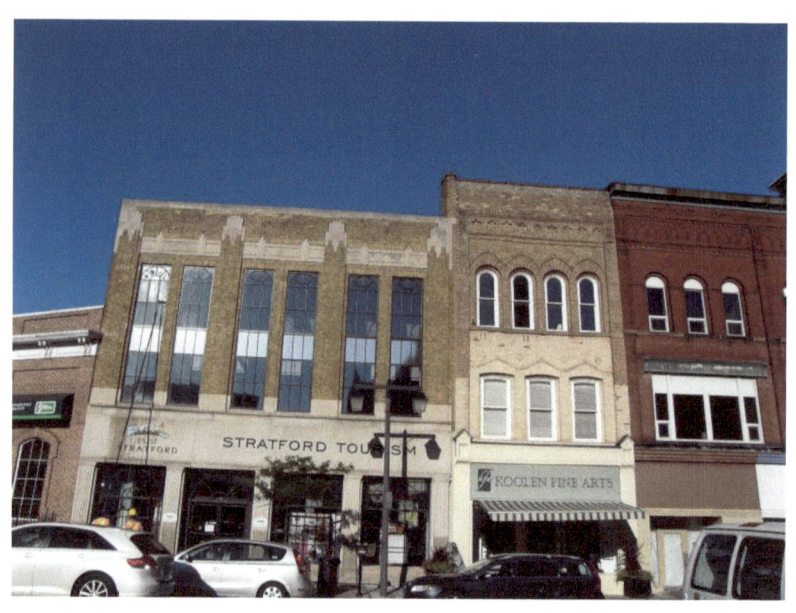

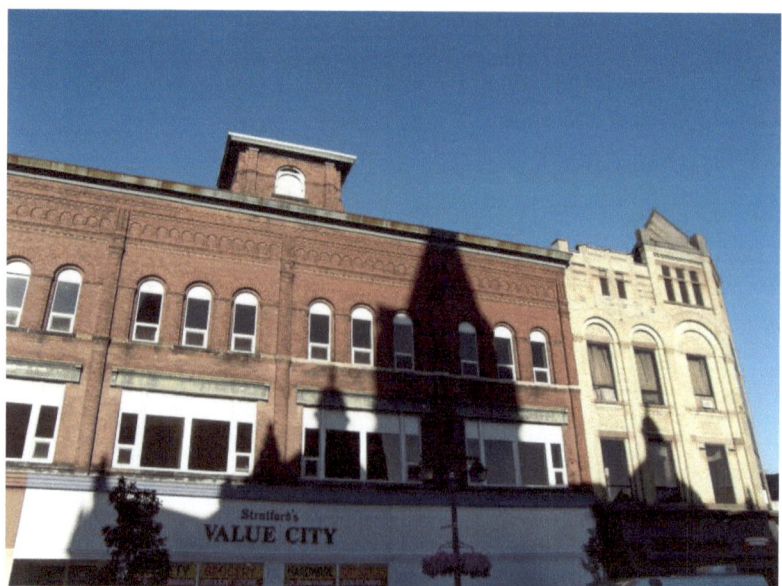

Decorative brickwork

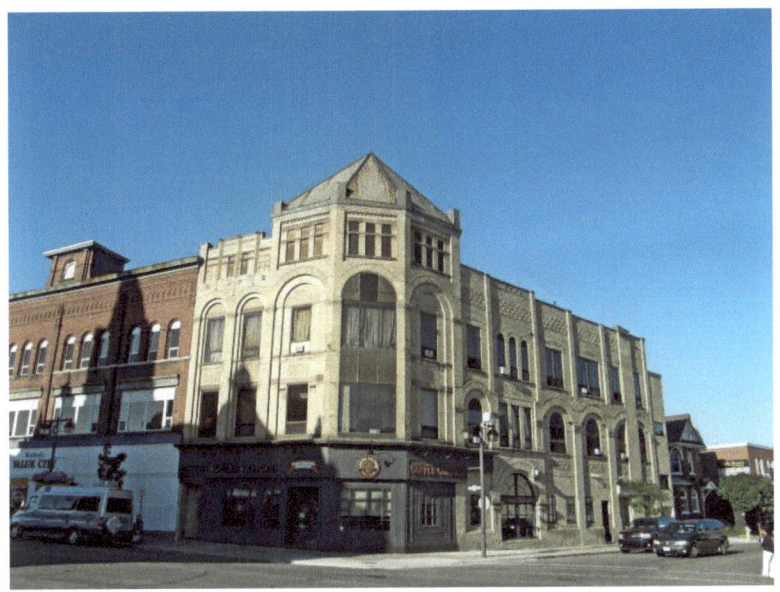

Romanesque round-arched windows

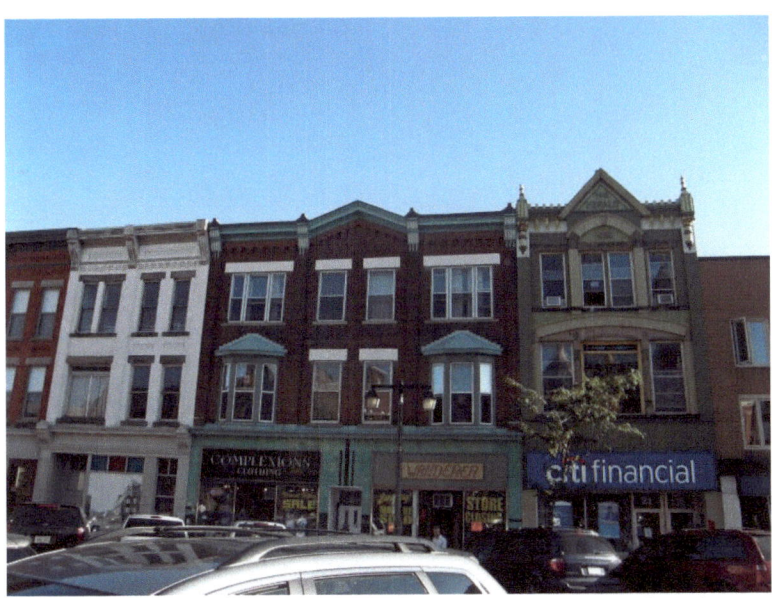

Cornice brackets, The Herald 1890, decorative brickwork

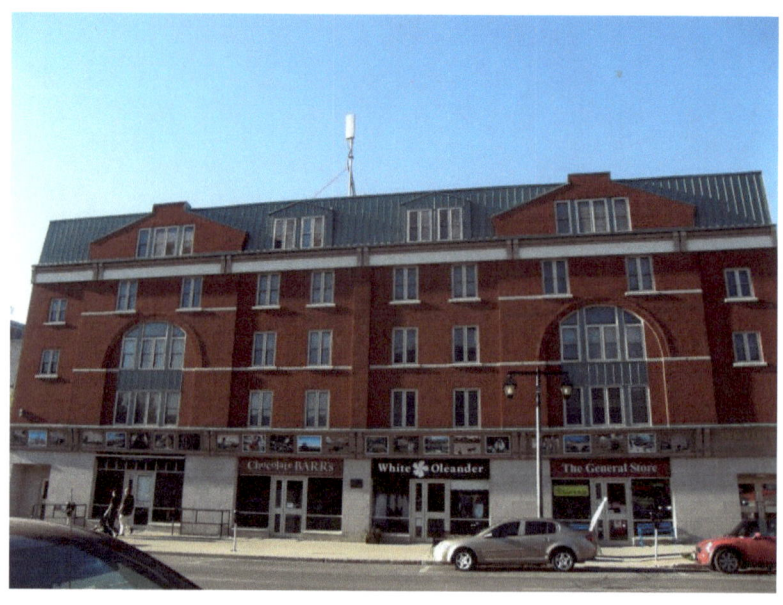

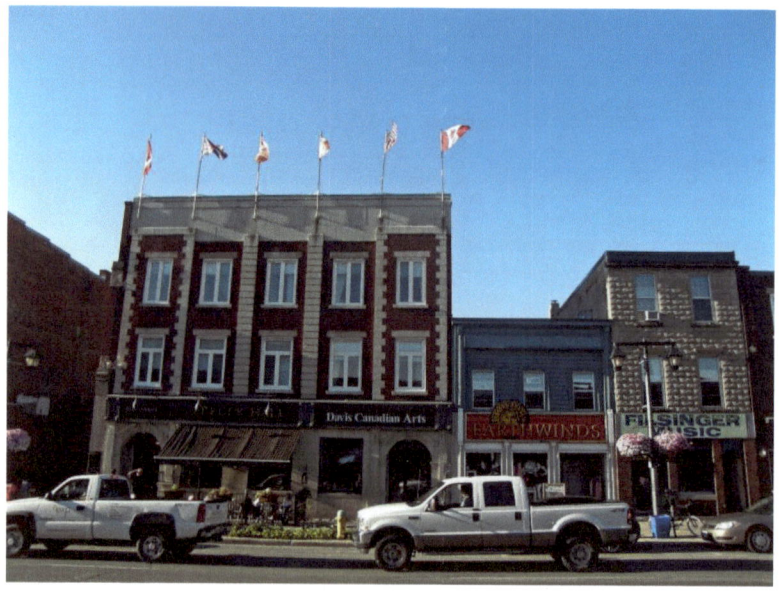

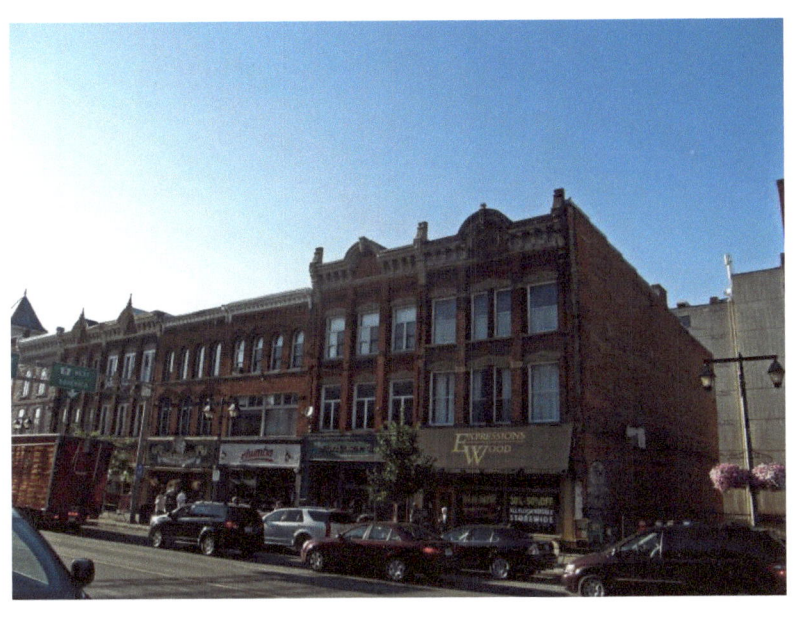

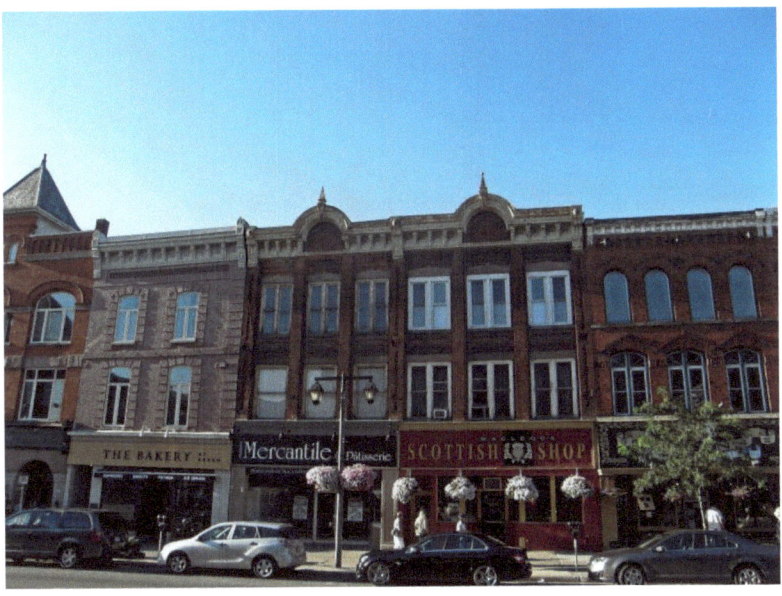

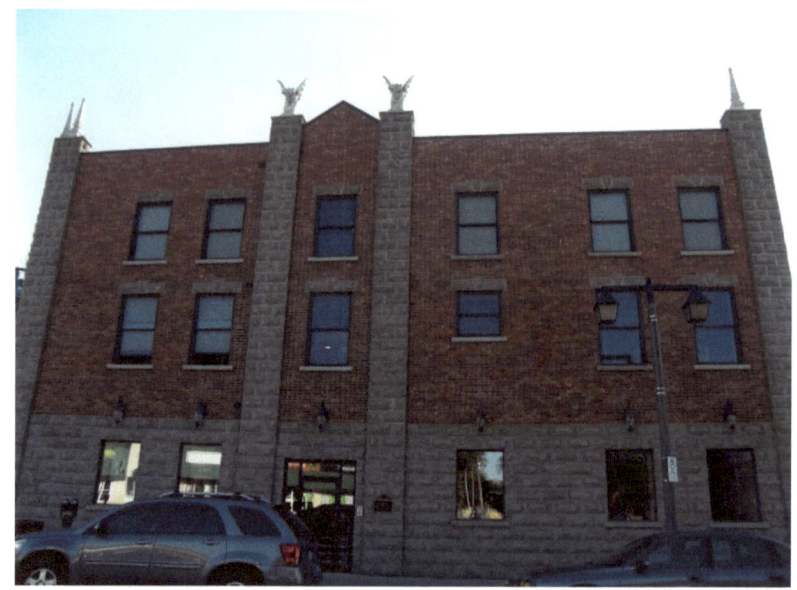

164 Downie Street – private residences

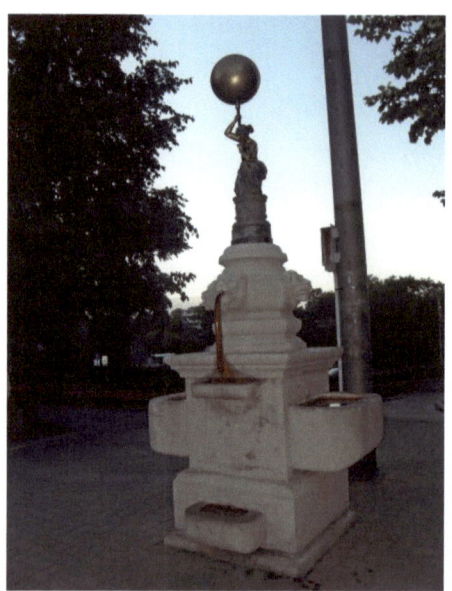

The Freeland Fountain is in memory of W.J. Freeland who came to the city in 1886 as the first supervisor of music in the public schools. He was renowned for his ability to draw out his pupils' voices and to teach them to sing by note. Freeland's charity towards animals is evident with the watering troughs at different levels for horses, dogs and humans.

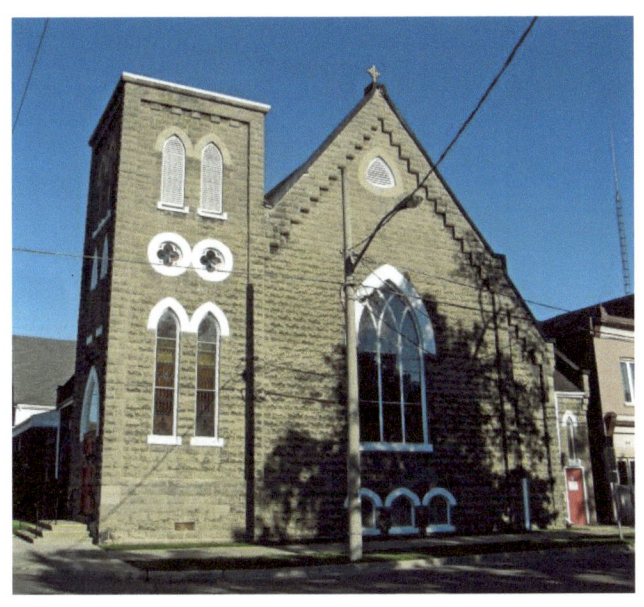

9 Douro Street - St. Paul's Anglican Church
Bell tower, lancet windows

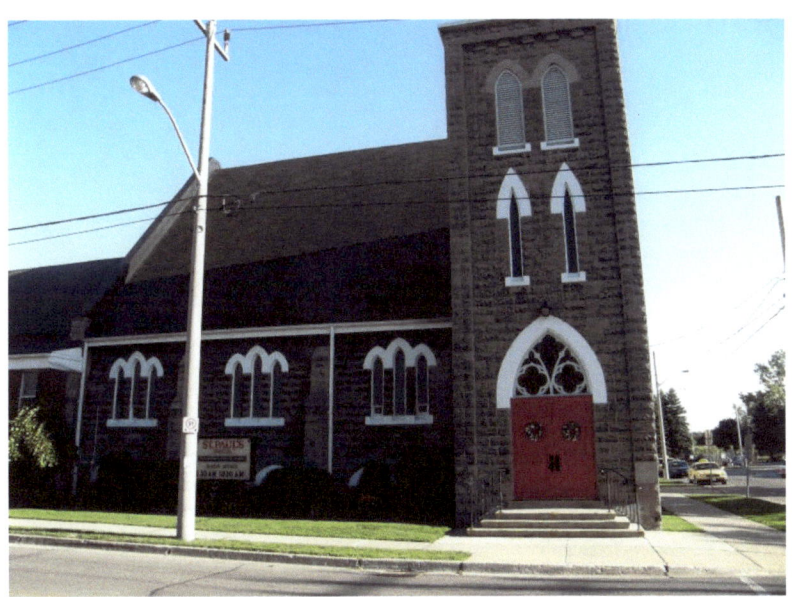

Buttresses

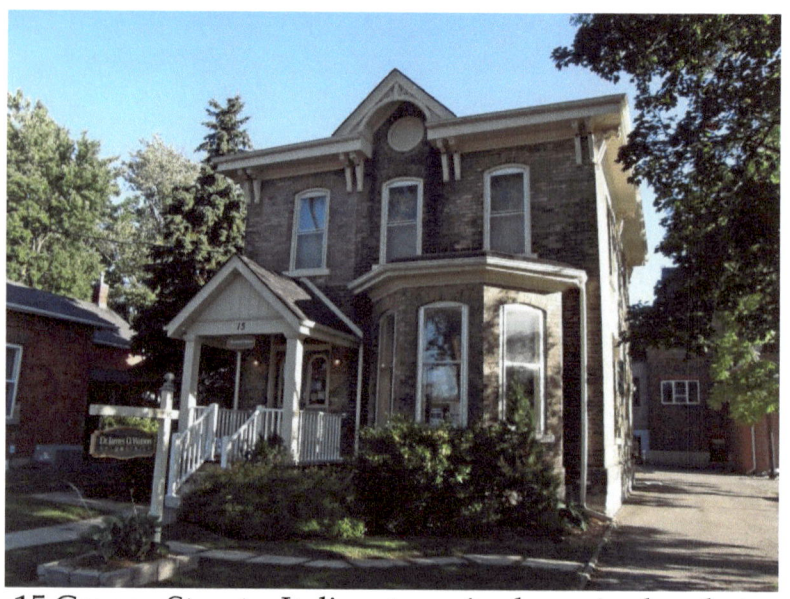

15 Grange Street – Italianate, paired cornice brackets, ground-floor bay window

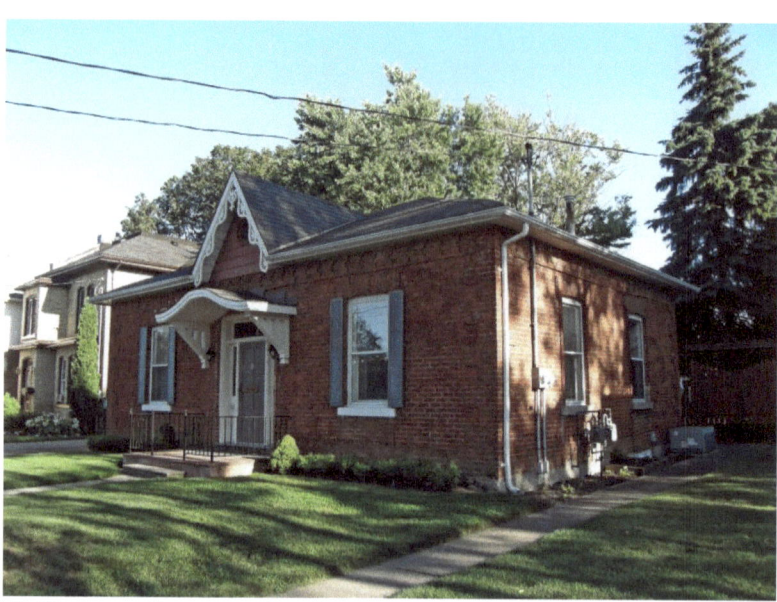

19 Grange Street – Gothic cottage, bargeboard on gable, decorative brickwork below the cornice, corner quoins

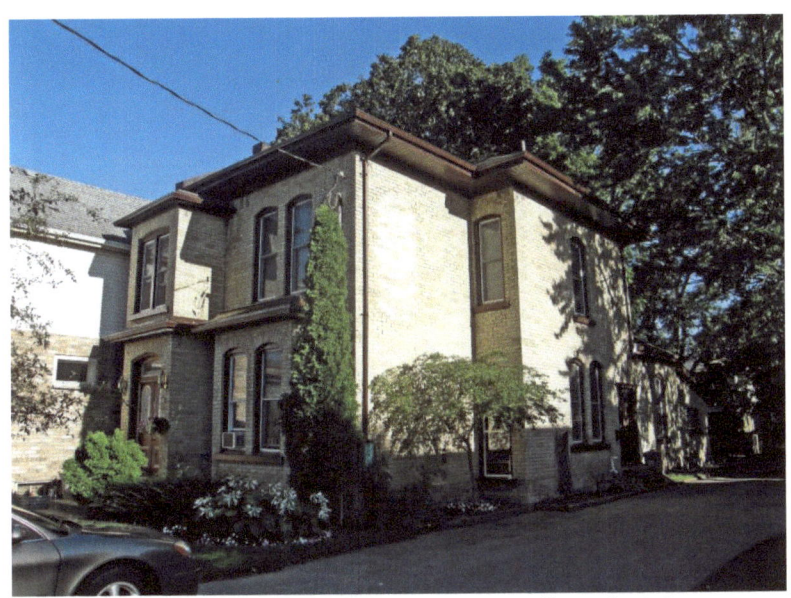

Grange Street – Italianate – yellow brick,
arched window voussoirs

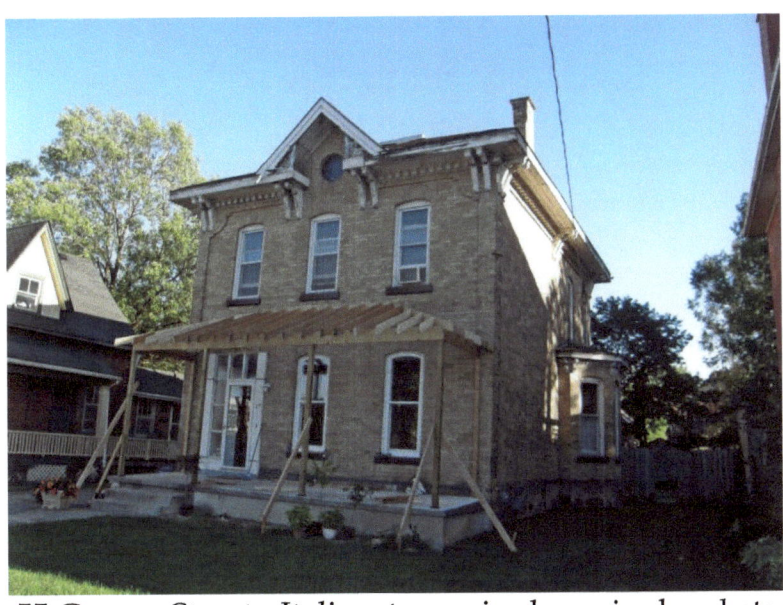

55 Grange Street - Italianate – paired cornice brackets
– yellow brick, dentil moulding below cornice

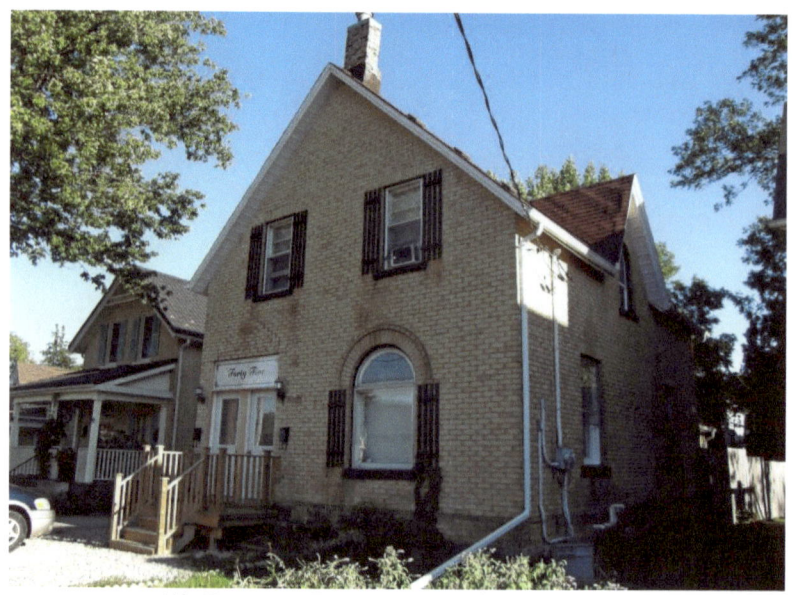

45 Grange Street – Gothic Revival

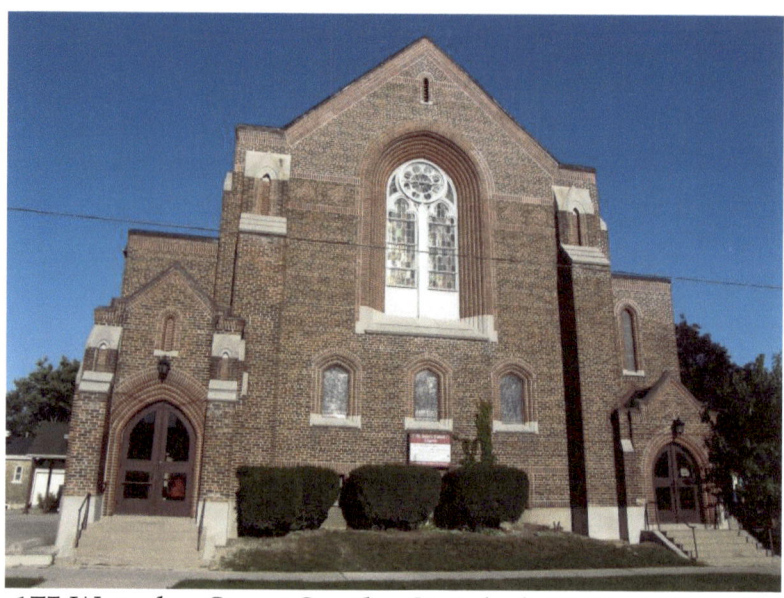

175 Waterloo Street South - St. John's United Church, rose window

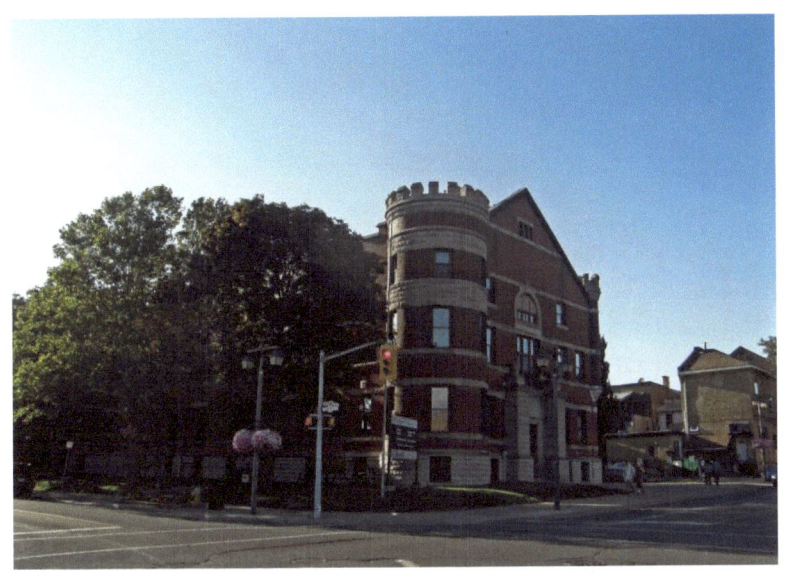

80 Waterloo Street – Armoury – Baronial Gothic Style – crenulated towers

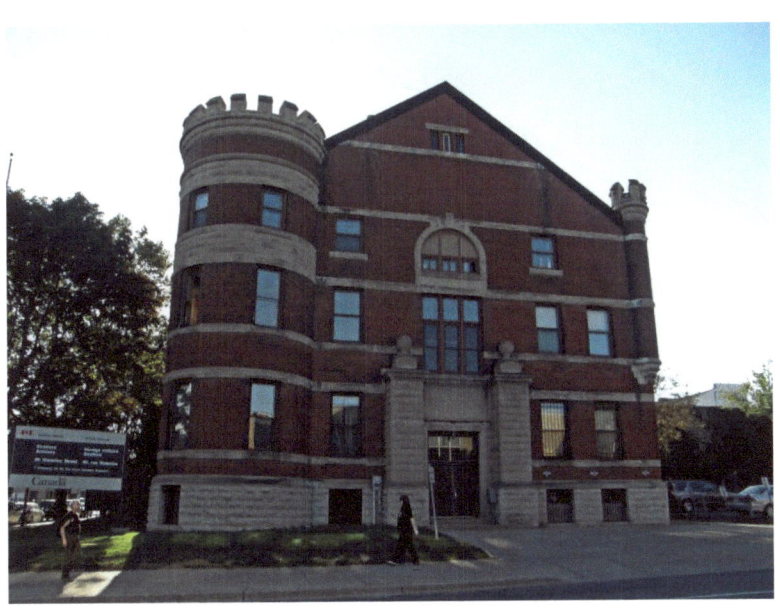

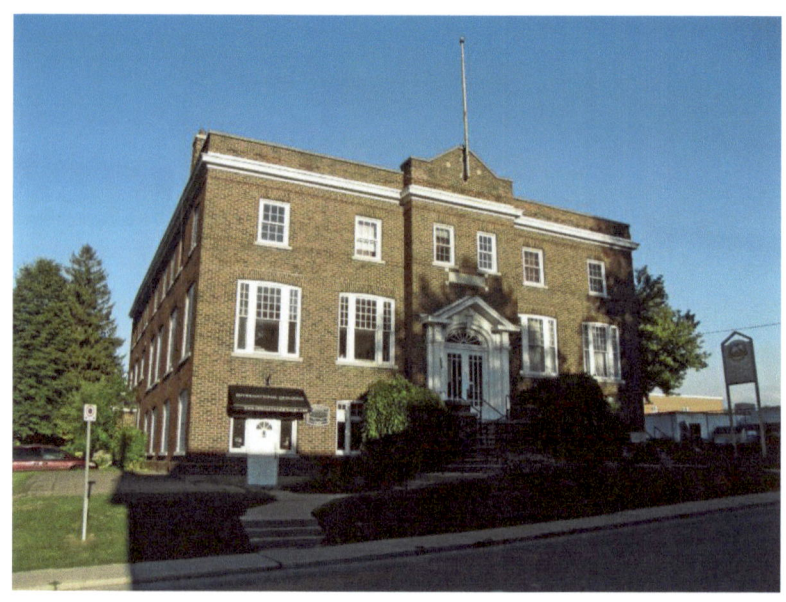

45 Waterloo Street – original YWCA building constructed in 1928 in red brick; now Nancy Campbell Collegiate Institute

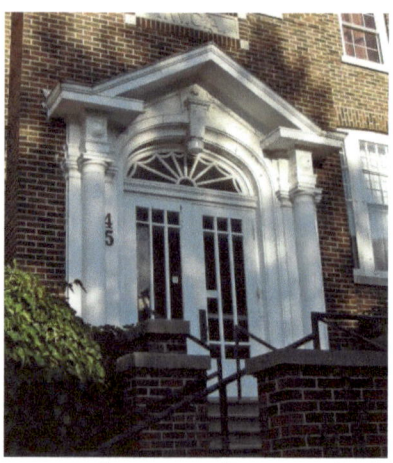

Pediment over door, sunburst window, finial

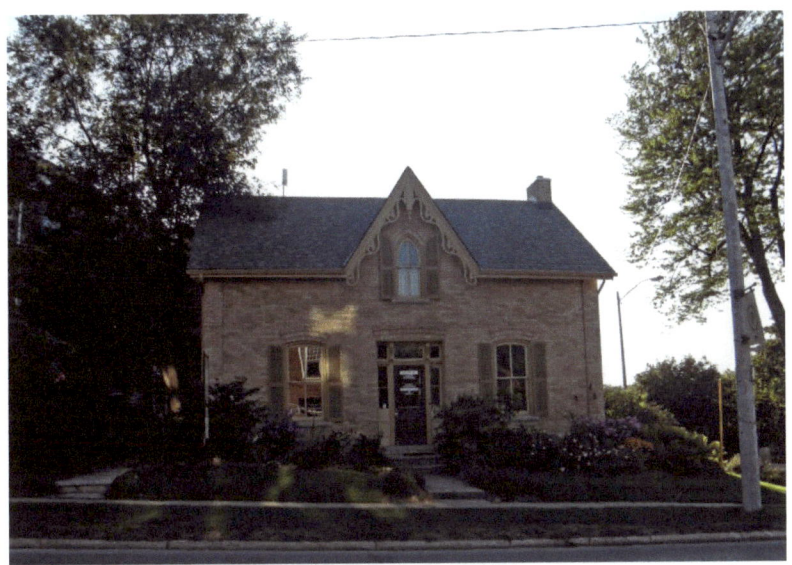

42 Waterloo Street – 1874 Gothic style, gable over door, decorative wood trim (bargeboard)

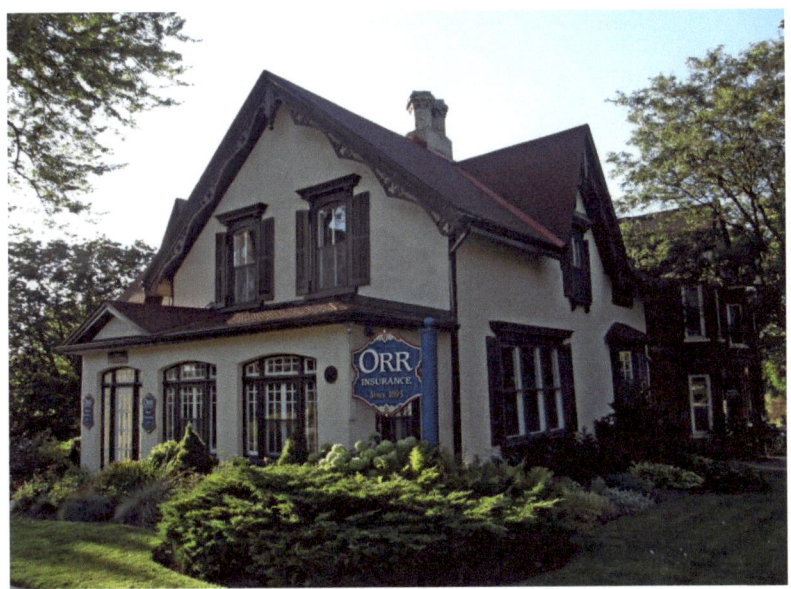

50 Cobourg Street – Gothic c. 1874 – Vergeboard trim, finials, upper windows are original with bracketed lintels

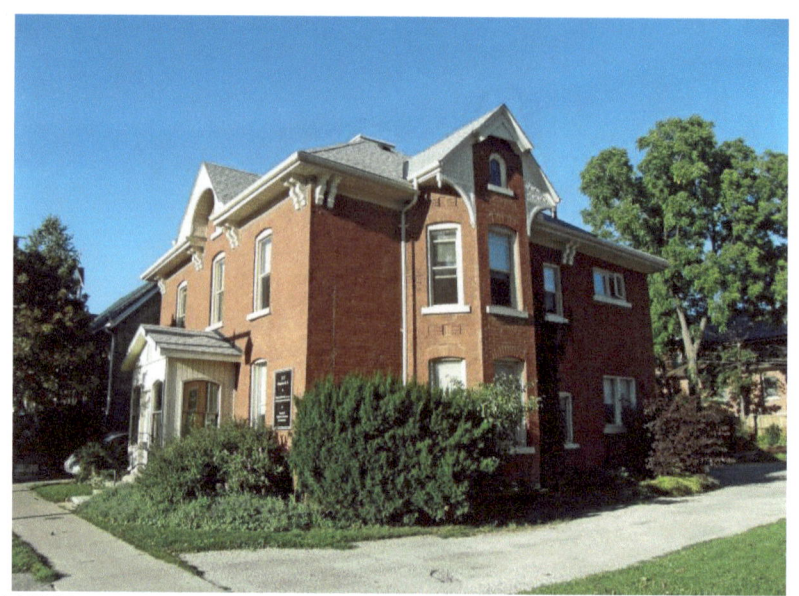

117 Victoria Street South – 2½ storey tower-like bay with fretwork brackets

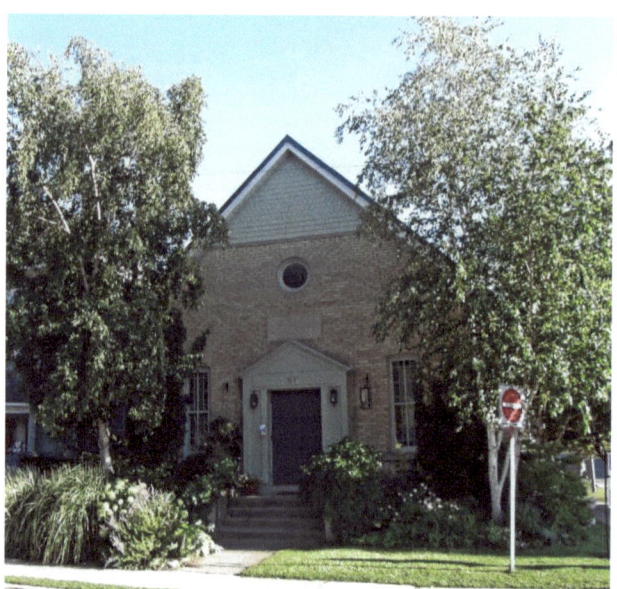

67 Brunswick Street

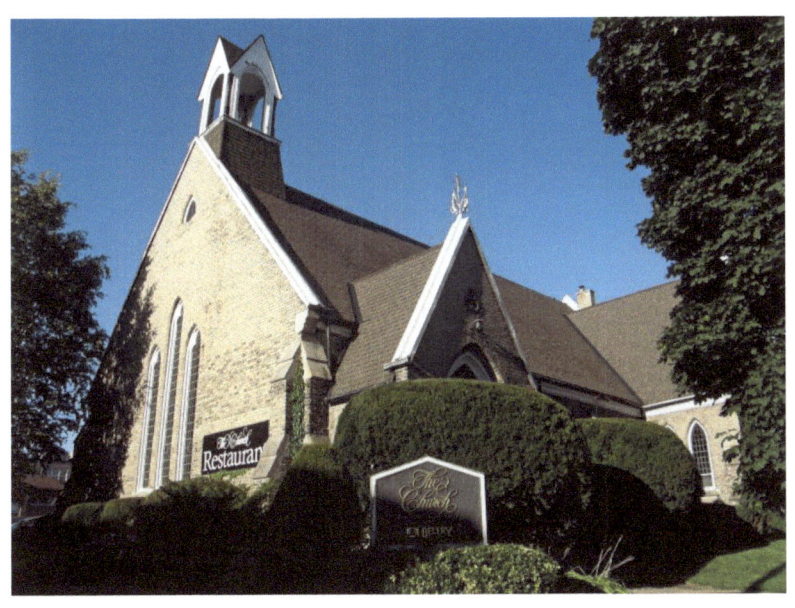

70 Brunswick Street

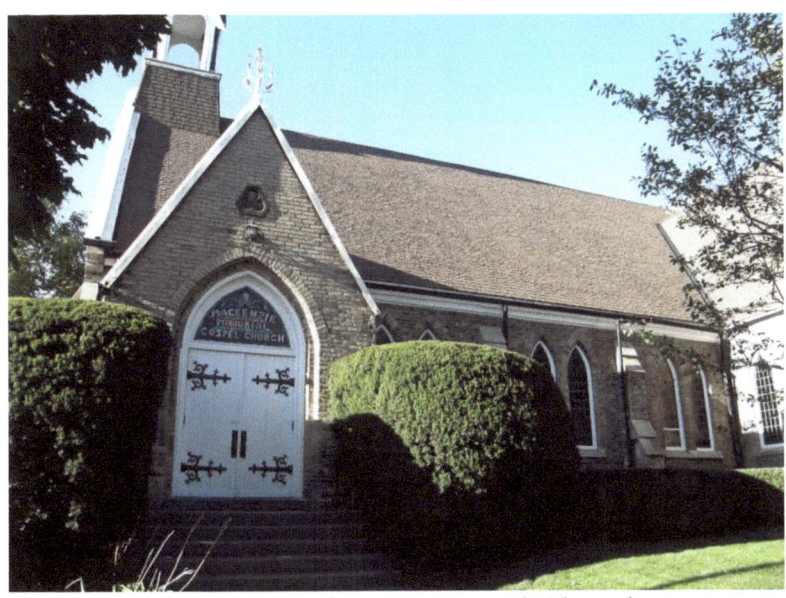

Former Mackenzie Gospel Church

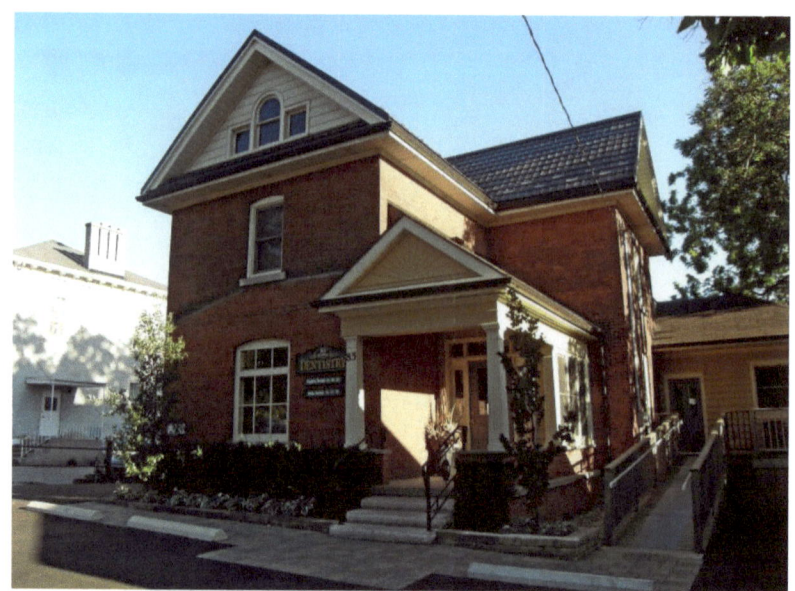

83 Brunswick Street – Edwardian style - Palladian window, triangular pediment above door

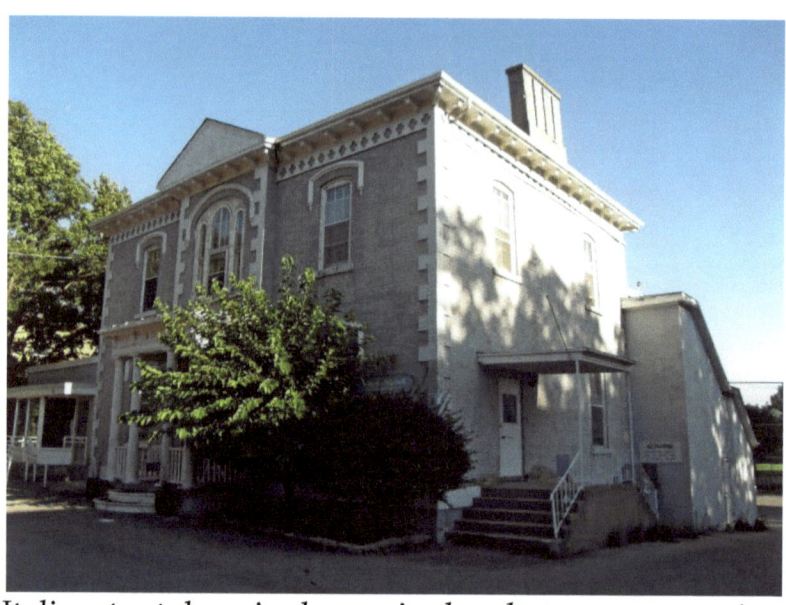

Italianate style – single cornice brackets, corner quoins, decorative brickwork under cornice

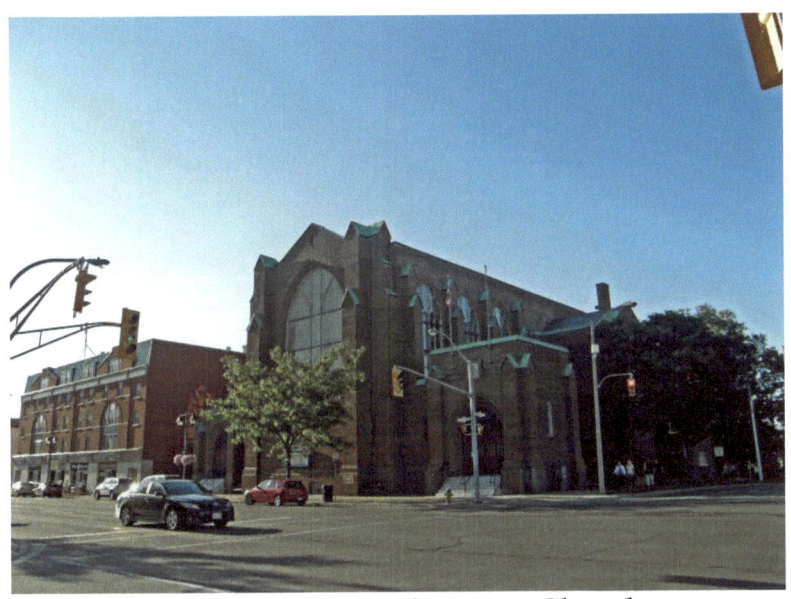

142 Ontario Street - Knox Presbyterian Church constructed
1913-1915 – Gothic Revival

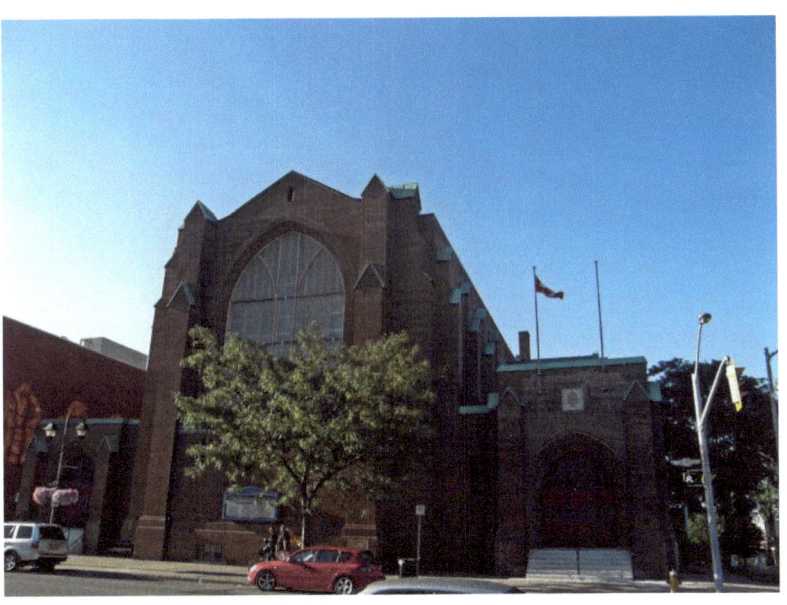

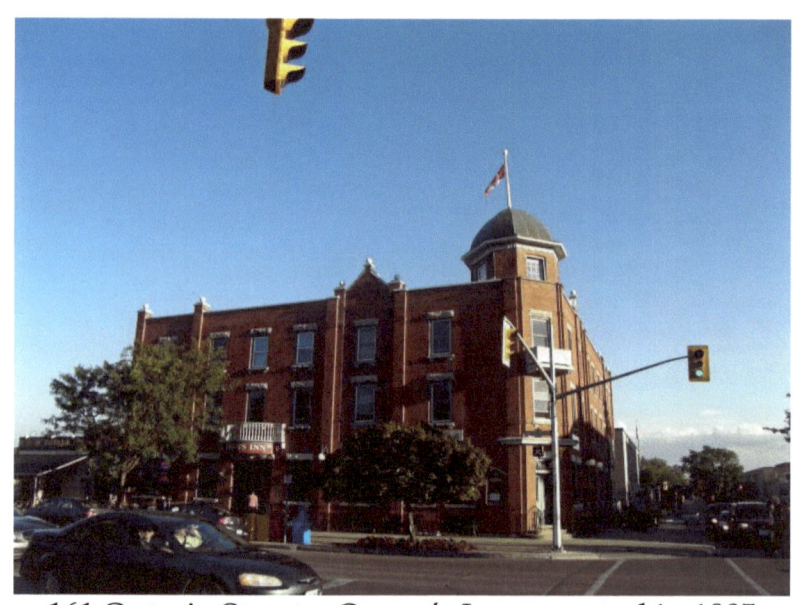

161 Ontario Street – Queen's Inn – erected in 1905
Neo-Classical Revival Style, cupola on top, pilasters

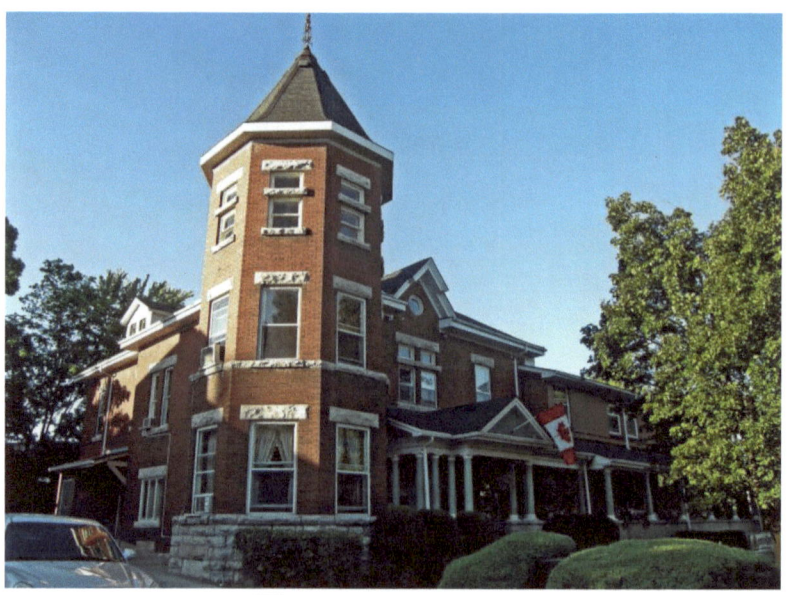

Three-storey turret

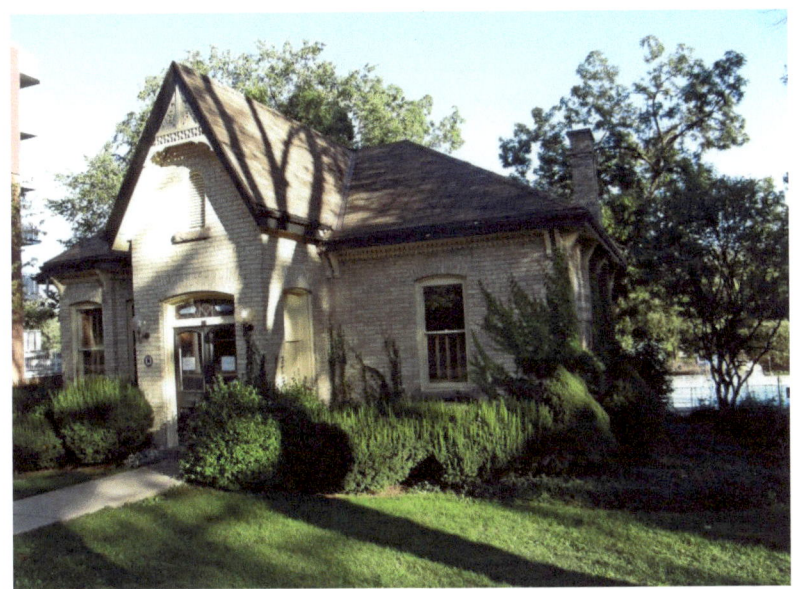

Ontario Street – Gothic Cottage, Vergeboard trim

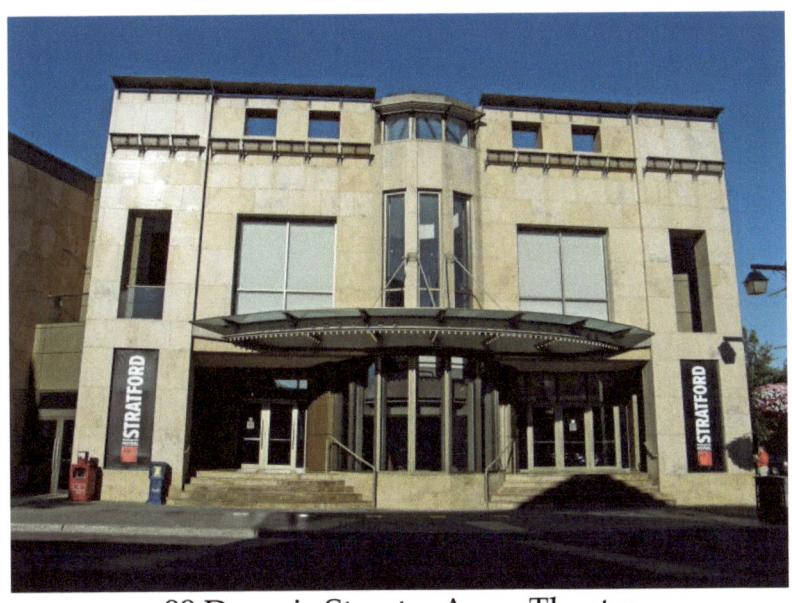

99 Downie Street – Avon Theatre

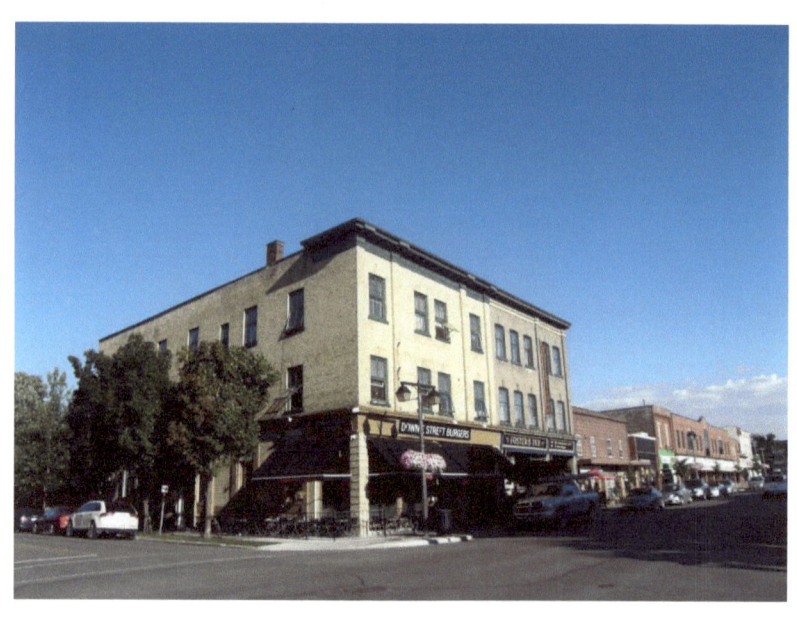

Downie Street

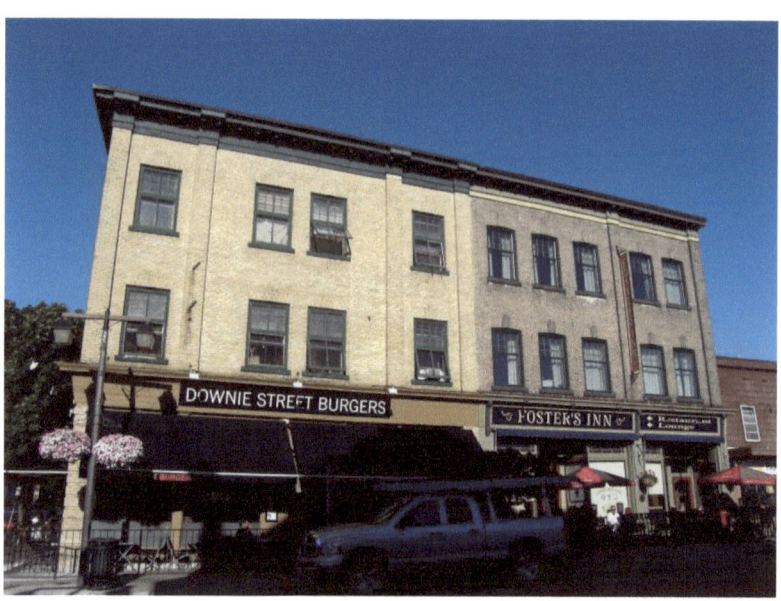

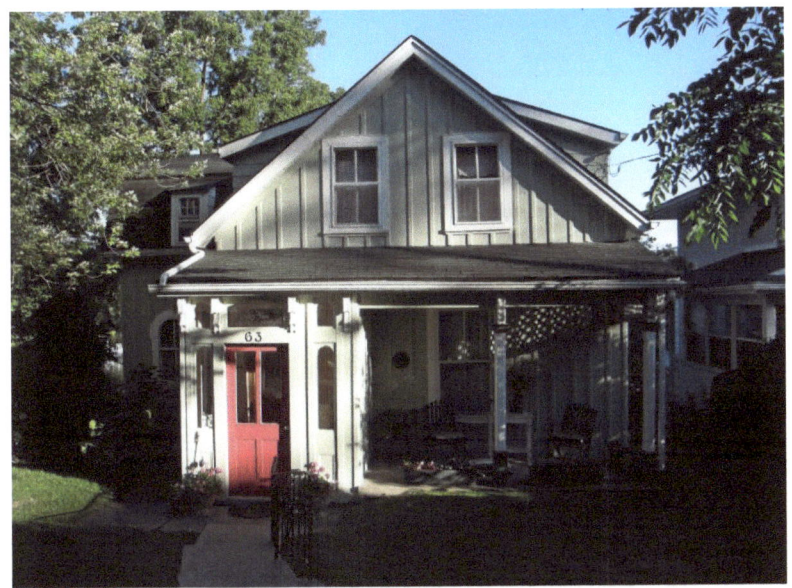

63 William Street – Todd/Gaudy House c. 1875
– Gothic Revival style, early board and batten house

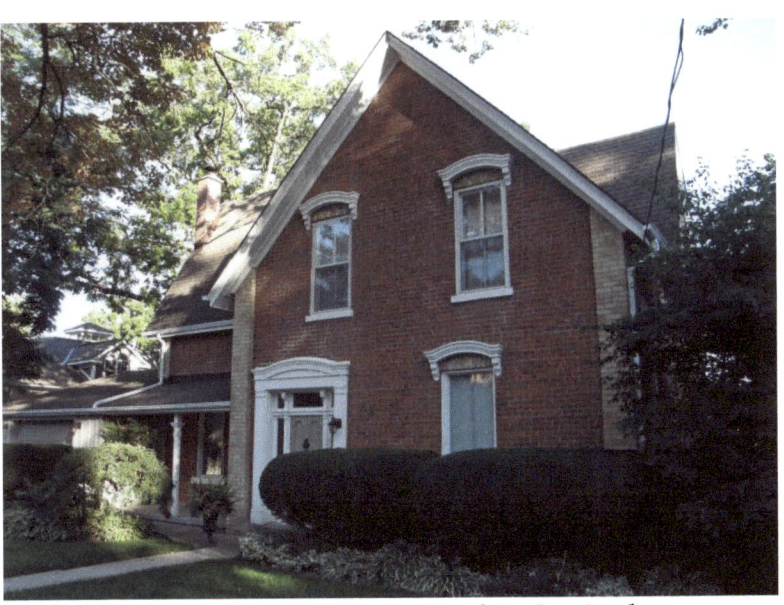

89 William Street – Gothic Revival

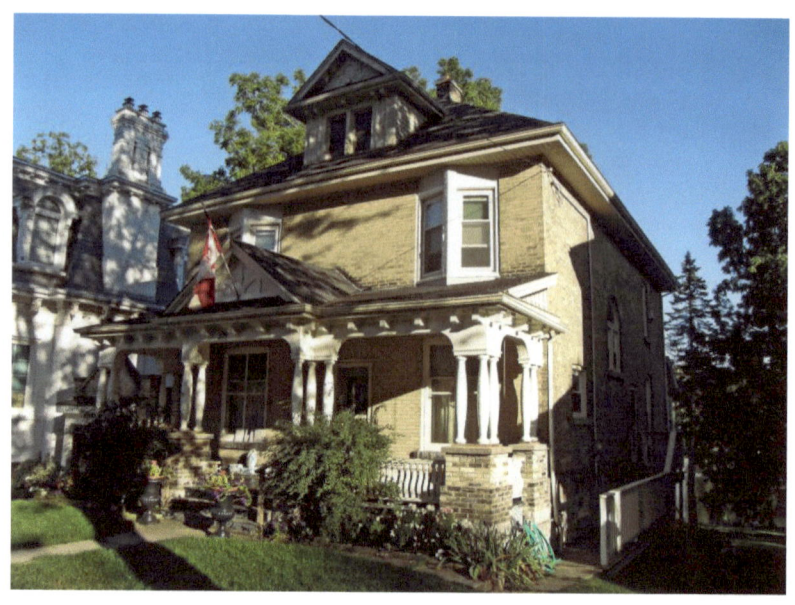

109 William Street – Italianate style – dormer in attic,
pediment above door, cornice brackets

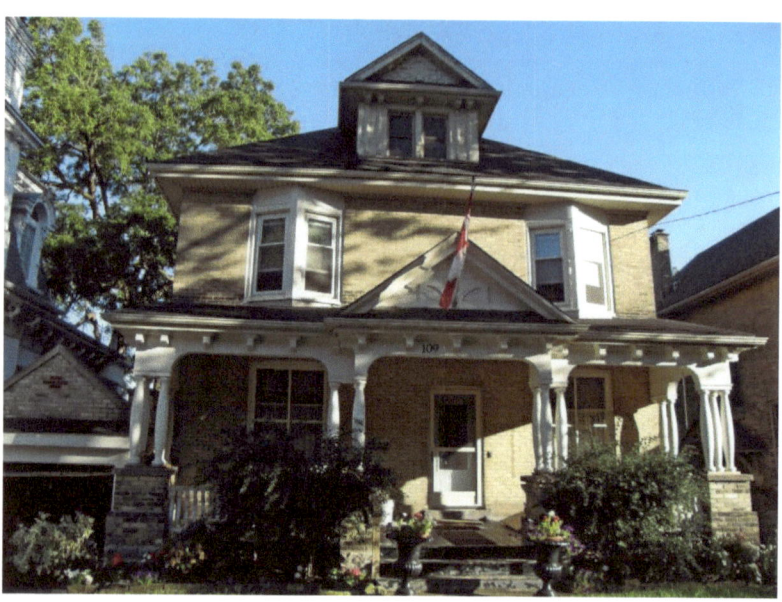

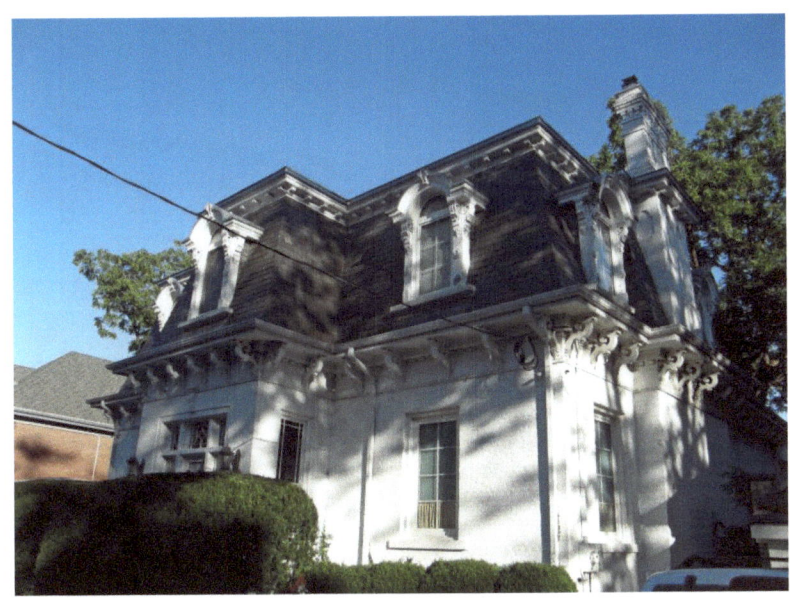

113 William Street – Second Empire style, mansard roof with dormers, cornice brackets, elaborately decorated window frames

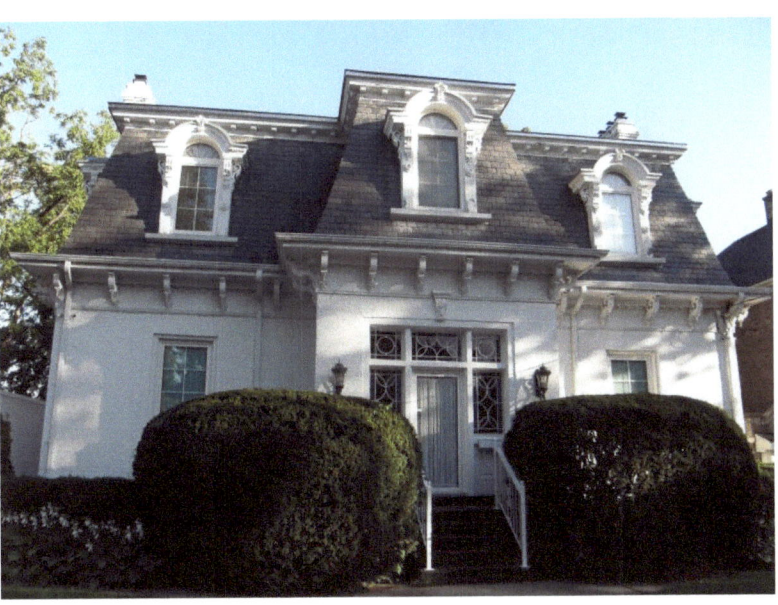

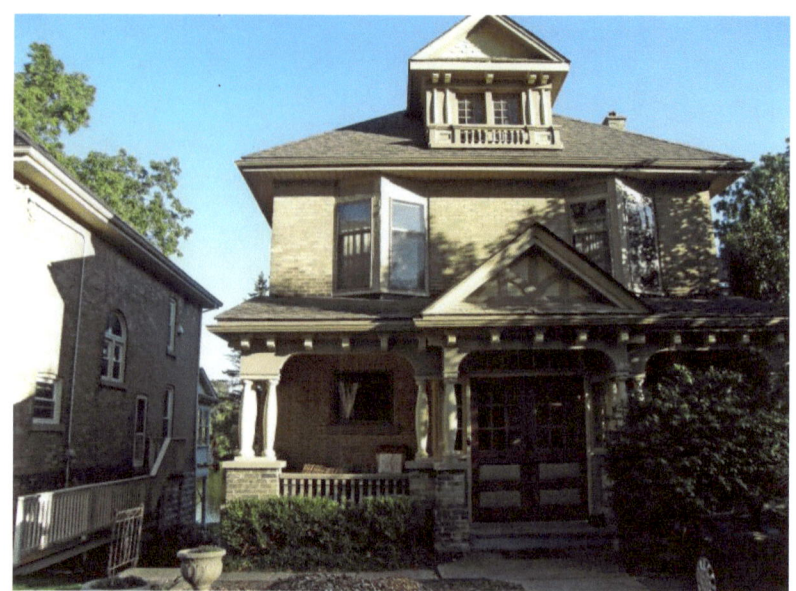

101 William Street – Italianate – dormer in attic, pediment above door, cornice brackets

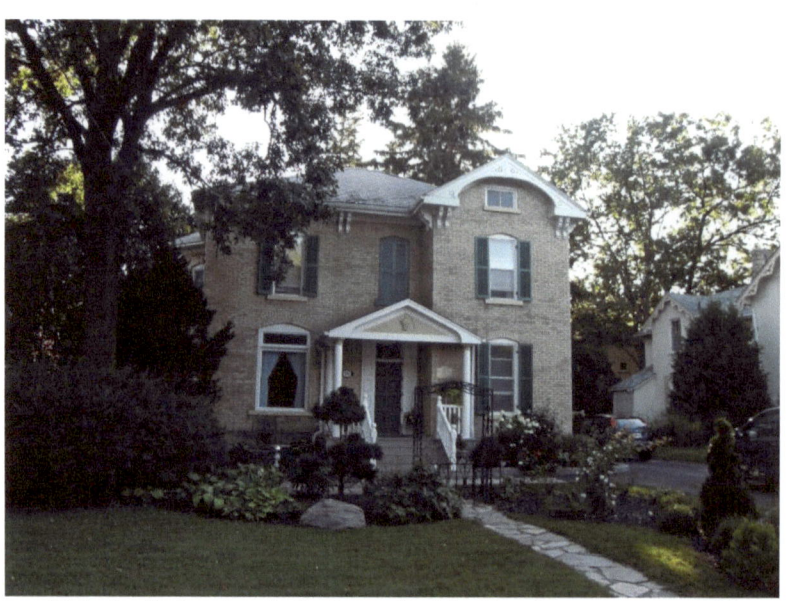

#54 – built for Annie Sydney-Smith, Gentlewoman in 1889
– Italianate with two-and-a-half storey tower-like bay, paired cornice brackets, Vergeboard trim on gable,
pediment above doorway

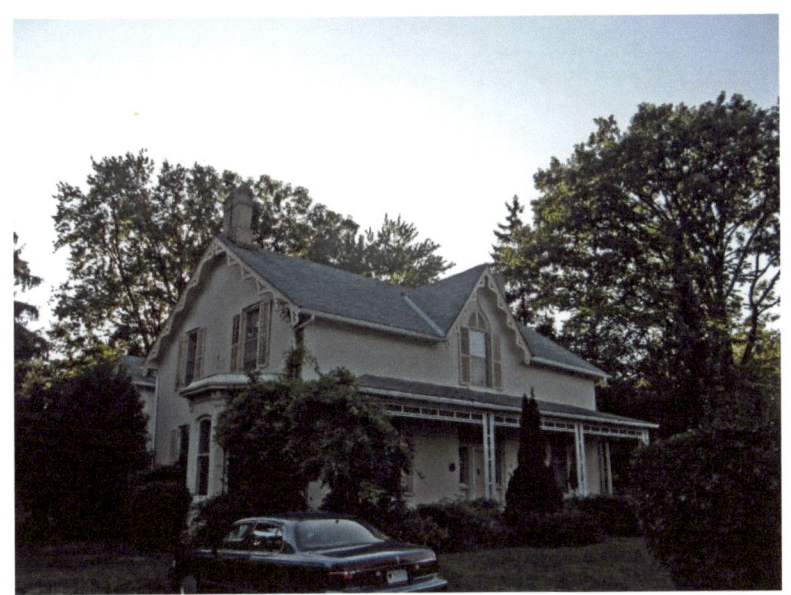

72 - John Sydney-Smith House c. 1859 – Gothic Revival,
Vergeboard trim on gables

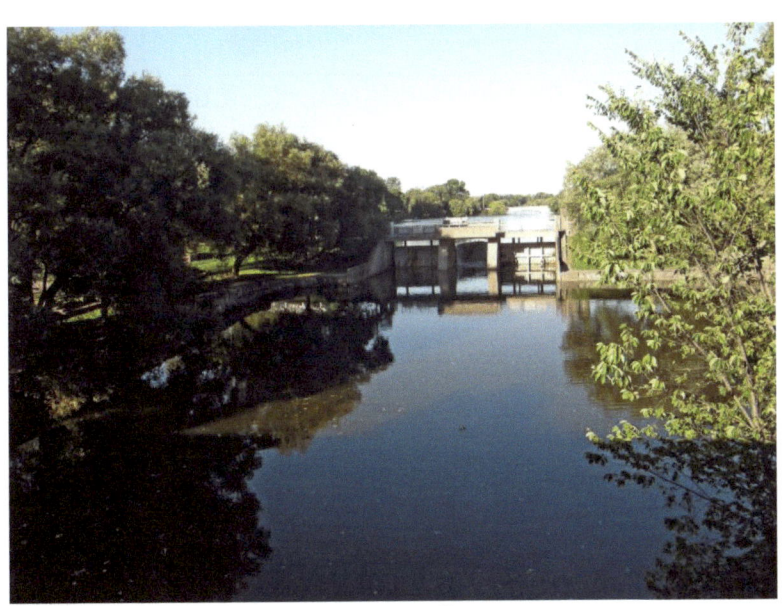

Avon River reflections

Bichromal masonry: is multi-coloured Example: Perth County Court House	
Buttress: a masonry structure built against or projecting from a wall which serves to support or reinforce the wall. In Canadian architecture, they are sometimes used for decoration. Example: St. James' Anglican Church	
Brackets: a decorative or weight-bearing structural element which forms a right angle with one side against a wall and the other under a projecting surface such as an eave or roof. Example: 53 Mornington Street	
Cornice: originally the wooden overhang of the roof. With the use of stone, brick, iron and steel, the cornice is any projecting shelf at the top of a ceiling or roof. They can be very decorative. Example: 53 Mornington Street	
Cornice Return: decorative element on the end of a gable. Example: 109 Mornington Street	
Dichromatic brickwork: the use of two colours of brick, tile or slate to decorate a façade. Example: 81 Ontario Street	

Dormer: (French for "sleep") a gable end window that pierces through the plane of a sloping roof surface to create usable space in the top floor or attic of a building by adding headroom. Example: 21 St. Andrew Street	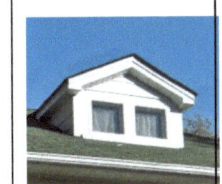
Finial: ornament added to the top of a gable, pinnacle, canopy or spire – a Gothic element. Example: 67 Caledonia Street	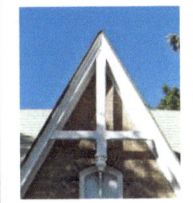
Fretwork: interlaced decorative design resembling a bracket Example: 117 Victoria Street South	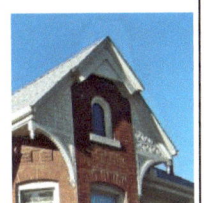
Gable: the triangular portion of a wall between the edges of a sloping roof. Example: 122 Mornington Street – triple gable	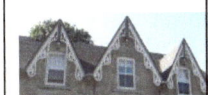
Hipped Roof: a roof where all sides slope downwards to the walls with no gables. Example: 160 Mornington Street	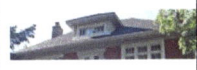
Keystones and Voussoirs: a voussoir is a wedge-shaped element used in building an arch. A keystone is the central stone that locks all the stones into position, allowing the arch to bear weight. A keystone is often enlarged and embellished. Example: 108 Mornington Street	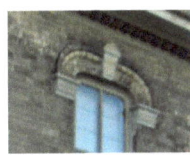

Lancet Window: a tall, narrow window with a pointed arch at its top. Example: St. James' Anglican Church	
Palladian Window: a large window that is divided into three sections with the centre section larger than the two side sections and usually arched.	
Pediment: a triangular section above the horizontal structure (entablature), typically supported by columns. The inside of the triangle is called the tympanum. Example: 101 William Street	
Quoin: masonry blocks at the corner of a wall, often a decorative feature, usually larger or of a different colour than the rest of the wall. Example: Perth County Court House	
Rustication: is an architectural feature where the masonry is usually squared-off but left with a rough outer surface and wide joints that emphasize the edges of each block. Rustication is often used to give visual weight to the ground floor. Example: Perth County Court House	

A **Sunburst** consists of rays or "beams" radiating out from a central disk in the manner of sunbeams. Sometimes part of a sunburst, a semicircular or semi-elliptical shape, is used. Traditional sunburst motifs usually show the rays narrowing as they get further from the center. In architecture, the sunburst is often used in window designs, including fanlights and rose windows, as well as in decorative motifs. Example: 45 Waterloo Street	
Transom: is a horizontal crosspiece separating a door from a window above it. Example: Perth County Court House	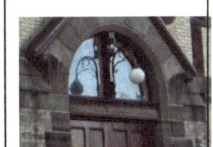
Turret: a small tower that projects from the wall of a building. Example: 76 William Street	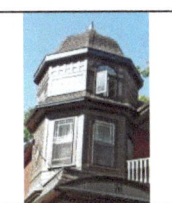
Vergeboards: also called bargeboards (gingerbread) – hang from the projecting end of a roof and are often elaborately carved and ornamented. Example: 122 Mornington Street	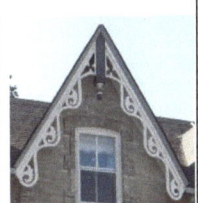

Edwardian, 1900-1930 – This style bridges the ornate and elaborate styles of the Victorian era and the simplified styles of the 20th century. Balanced facades, simple roof lines, dormer windows, large front porches, and smooth brick surfaces are its characteristics. Example: 83 Brunswick Street	
Gothic Revival, 1830-1890 – These decorative buildings have sharply-pitched gables with highly detailed vergeboards, pointed-arch window openings, and dichromatic brickwork. It is a common style in Ontario. Example: 122 Mornington Street	
Italianate, 1850-1900 – It has wide-bracketed eaves, belvederes, wrap-around verandahs. Example: 109 Mornington Street	
Neo-classical, or "new" classical – buildings inspired by ancient Greece and Rome. Symmetrical shape, tall columns that rise the full height of the building, triangular pediment, domed roof, elliptical fanlight above door and sidelights. Example: Stratford Public Library, 19 St. Andrews Street	

Queen Anne, 1885-1900 – This style is distinguished by an irregular outline featuring a combination of an offset tower, broad gables, projecting two-storey bays, verandahs, multi-sloped roofs, and tall, decorative chimneys. A mixture of brick and wood is common. Windows often have one large single-paned bottom sash and small panes in the upper sash. Example: 76 Mornington Street	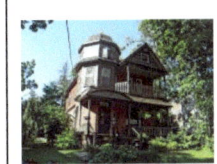
Romanesque Revival, 1880-1910 – This style hearkens back to medieval architecture of the 11th and 12th centuries with a heavy appearance, blocky towers and rounded arches. Example: Perth County Court House	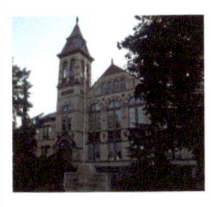

www.ingramcontent.com/pod-product-compliance
Lightning Source LLC
Chambersburg PA
CBHW040836180526
45159CB00001B/209